A Human Rights Handbook for Judges and Lawyers

Foreword

Santiago A. Canton
Secretary-General, International Commission of Jurists,
Geneva, Switzerland

As Secretary-General of the International Commission of Jurists, I welcome the publication of this *Human Rights Handbook for Judges and Lawyers*, written by our long-time Honorary Commissioner and friend, Bertrand Ramcharan.

Upholding human rights is at the heart of the judicial function, and of the mission of lawyers. The challenges of the judicial enforcement of human rights are growing in a world of catastrophic climate change, environmental deterioration, unfettered use of artificial intelligence, stalled implementation of the UN Sustainable Development Goals, persistent global poverty and inequality, systematic gross violations of human rights committed without accountability or redress, and a declining number of genuine democracies grounded in the rule of law.

The International Commission of Jurists (ICJ) is a non-governmental organization of leading judges and lawyers from around the world working to advance the rule of law and realization of human rights for all. Our vision is of "A just society governed by the rule of law where all people equally enjoy their human rights."

The Commissioners are 60 eminent judges and lawyers – from all parts of the world and all legal systems. They are selected for their experience, knowledge and fundamental commitment to human rights. They support the work of our legal teams to strengthen and implement international standards, improving legislation that has positively impacted the lives of millions of people.

We work globally to implement our mandate, with legal advisors based in the countries or regions that they cover, and offices in Geneva (Switzerland), Brussels (Belgium), Bangkok (Thailand), Tunis (Tunisia) and Kathmandu (Nepal) with individual presences in various other countries.

The ICJ is convinced that despite the retrogressive global tendences, the rule of law and human rights law and standards must remain at the heart of approaches for the preservation and advancement of humanity. They can and must be developed and harnessed so as to effectively contribute to addressing the great challenges to human life and dignity of our times, including catastrophic climate change and the adverse effects of new digital technologies, especially as applied to communications, artificial intelligence, and surveillance.

To this end, the ICJ has affirmed since its founding more than 70 years ago that judges, lawyers and prosecutors have a paramount role in safeguarding human rights and the rule of law, and that this responsibility is particularly pronounced in times of crisis and instability.

In this Handbook, Bertie, magnificently shares with us all his knowledge and experience of a lifetime working to advance human rights and the rule of law throughout the world. His experience working with the UN, civil society organizations and academia, provide to us a unique point of view that is extremely useful in today´s complex world. The Handbook succinctly assembles materials and insights that can be of great assistance to judges and lawyers worldwide in their own efforts to secure human rights and the rule of law.

It commences with a recapitulation of the challenges to judges and lawyers in contributing to the achievement of UN Sustainable Development Goal No. 16, which deals with the importance of working for just, peaceful and inclusive societies worldwide. It then proceeds to discuss the need for an adequate and effective national human rights protection system in every country – something that judges would do well to keep in mind.

It summarises for the benefit of the legal community, the legal obligations of every State under the UN Charter, as well the legal obligations of States parties to human rights treaties that they have committed themselves to. It then outlines the UN Basic Principles on the Right to a Remedy and Reparation for Victims of Gross Violations of Human Rights. Thereafter, it presents the UN Basic Principles on the Independence of the Judiciary.

It then offers a concise summary of universally-binding human rights law and standards, on which it follows up by offering, in an Appendix, an innovative Recapitulation of Core Universally-Binding Human Rights Norms.

It is sensible and practical, and I commend it to the legal community and more broadly to human rights defenders everywhere.

Foreword

Dr. Francisco Rojas Aravena
Rector of the University for Peace, San José, Costa Rica

Inspired by the philosophy of the United Nations Charter and the Universal Declaration of Human Rights, the University for Peace (UPEACE) has been striving, ever since its establishment, to promote a culture of peace and justice, grounded in respect for human dignity and rights, and in universal implementation of the right to development.

Created in pursuance of UN General Assembly Resolution 35/55 in 1980, UPEACE has been training leaders for peace for the past five decades. It is a unique global academic institution with over 6,000 Alumni hailing from more than 120 nations working for peace on a global scale. UPEACE is a unique institution within the United Nations system mandated exclusively for peace education. UPEACE's unique attributes lie in its specialized UN mandate, global community, interdisciplinary curriculum, commitment to practical learning, and emphasis on sustainable development.

Sustainable Development Goal 16 has provided a noble framework for these efforts. SDG 16 aims to promote peaceful and inclusive societies for sustainable development, provide access to justice for all, and build effective, accountable and inclusive institutions at all levels. SDG 16 envisages the rule of law at the national and international levels and ensuring equal access to justice for all. Compassion and a strong moral compass are essential to every democratic society.

UPEACE heartily welcomes the publication of this *Human Rights Handbook for Judges and Lawyers*, written by a respected member of the UN family, Dr Bertrand Ramcharan, First Swiss Chair of Human Rights at the Geneva Graduate Institute, who joined the United Nations in 1973 and has continued to serve the causes of peace and human rights ever since.

He served the cause of peace as Director of the International Conference on the Former Yugoslavia, as Director of the Office of the SRSG in charge of all UN activities in the Former Yugoslavia: peace-making, peace-keeping, peacebuilding, and humanitarian activities; as Director in the UN Political Department; and as Special Adviser to the UN Secretary-General who undertook a special mission to Georgia on the eve of the conflict in that country. He has also performed the functions of UN High Commissioner for Human Rights. He is the author of various books, including: *Contemporary Preventive Diplomacy* and *Contemporary Human Rights Ideas.*

This *Human Rights Handbook* invites judges and lawyers to be mindful of the goals of SDG 16 in their quest to realize the rule of law worldwide, and to be guided by the international law of the UN Charter, the Universal Declaration of Human Rights, and solemn declarations related to the rule of law adopted by the United Nations such as on the independence of the judiciary and on principles of remedies and reparations.

This is a refreshing and innovative work on the implementation of the rule of law nationally, regionally, and internationally, and UPEACE heartily recommends it to the legal community, the peace community and the human rights community worldwide.

Preface

In my half a century of involvement with the international human rights cause and with international human rights law, I have come to think that perhaps the most important strategic concept for the universal realization of human rights and fundamental freedoms is that of the national human rights protection system – implementing legally-binding international human rights norms and national norms that are consistent with international law. A national human rights protection system has at least six dimensions: constitutional, legislative, judicial, preventive, protective, and educational.

Within a national human rights protection system, judges and lawyers have central roles. Put simply, the inhabitants of a country are entitled to be able to go to the courts to seek judicial enforcement of their rights. Lawyers normally initiate such actions, which are argued before judges. The more lawyers and judges have access to the content of international human rights law, the better the chances are that the cause of justice will be served when it comes to enforcement of the rights of individuals and groups.

In this *Human Rights Handbook for Judges and Lawyers,* my aim is to remind judges and lawyers that, under the United Nations Charter, every Government has legal obligations to uphold fundamental human rights, without discrimination, within, as well as outside, their jurisdictions. I recall for the attention of judges and lawyers that the international community has elevated some international human rights norms to the status of peremptory norms of international law, or norms of *jus cogens*. Among these are the absolute prohibition of slavery and of torture.

I draw attention to the fact that there are human rights norms of customary international law that are binding on every government, in accordance with the sources of international law enumerated in Article 38 of the Statute of the International Court of Justice. I offer a selection of human rights in the Universal Declaration of Human Rights that have now attained the status of customary international law. My point here is to remind judges and lawyers that they are entitled to hold Governments accountable to these norms of customary international law. This enumeration of human rights norms of customary international law is a pioneering and unique feature of the book.

Finally, I recall that judges are entitled to discover binding human rights norms in general principles of law that are shared by the principal legal systems of the world. The principle of non-discrimination is surely one such general principle of law.

This Handbook does not aim to be comprehensive. My goal has been to create an easily accessible and concise guide, offering a selection of core materials. My hope is that this offering will be of some assistance to judges and lawyers, as well as to other human rights practitioners. And it is my further hope that, over time, one might be able to update this presentation of binding international human rights norms that every government is obliged to abide by.

The story of human rights is one of shared efforts, step by step. I have been fortunate to have been associated with others in this quest over the past half a century.

Bertrand Ramcharan
Barrister/Attorney-at-Law, Georgetown, Guyana

1 The Challenges for Judges and Lawyers Worldwide: Just, Peaceful, and Inclusive Societies

1 Introduction

At the heart of the UN's 2030 Agenda for Sustainable Development lies a vision of a "just, equitable, tolerant, open and socially inclusive world in which the needs of the most vulnerable are met". *Justice for All*, a research report published by the Task Force on Justice, a group established by Pathfinders for Peaceful, Just and Inclusive Societies,[1] emphasises that without increased justice, the world will not be able to end poverty, reduce inequality, reach those left behind, create conditions for shared and sustainable prosperity, or promote peace and inclusion.

The third target of the UN's Sustainable Development Goal 16 (SDG 16) aims to ensure equal access to justice for all by 2030. Other justice-related targets cover legal identity, injustices such as corruption and illicit financial flows, and the promotion of human rights and gender equality. A people-centred approach to justice, the Pathfinders underlined, starts with an understanding of people's justice needs and by designing solutions to respond to them.

The Task Force on Justice studied the delivery of SDG 16 targets in a world where billions of people are not yet able to obtain justice. They assessed that 5.1 billion people – two thirds of the world's population – lack meaningful access to justice. The justice gap, they noted, is both a reflection of structural inequalities and a contributor to these inequalities.

The global justice gap, they think, has three dimensions: first, at least 253 million people live in extreme conditions of injustice. Of these, forty million people are in modern slavery; 12 million are stateless; and over 200 million live in countries or communities where high levels of insecurity make it impossible for them to seek justice.

Second, 1.5 billion people have justice problems that they cannot resolve. People in this group may be victims of unreported violence or crime; or they may have a civil or administrative justice problem that they cannot resolve, such as a dispute over land or the denial of a public service. The Pathfinders Task Force assessed that almost 60 percent of global justice problems are currently unresolved.

Third, 4.5 billion people are excluded from opportunities that the law

1 See Pathfinders, *Justice for All. The Task Force on Justice. Final Report* (2019) at http://www.justice.sdg16.plus.

provides. Over 1 billion people in the world lack legal identity. More than 2 billion are employed in the informal sector and the same number lack proof of housing or land tenure. This makes them vulnerable to abuse and exploitation and less able to access economic opportunities and public services.

The Task Force considered that by taking justice problems as a starting point, countries can design a better journey to solutions. In their view, a justice journey has three stages: first, people are empowered so that they can act when a legal need arises. They are helped to understand the law and seek a solution, with legal aid provided to the most vulnerable.

Second, people have access to services that are responsive to their needs and offer alternative and less adversarial pathways to justice. Third, people achieve a resolution to their problem that is fair and meets human rights standards. Remedies are appropriate and promote reconciliation. Data is used to judge whether people receive a satisfactory solution. Grievance mechanisms listen and respond to those who feel badly treated.

The Task Force on Justice stressed that justice systems must prevent problems as well as work to resolve those that have already occurred. Because it is forward-looking, prevention requires a transformation in justice systems. It requires the justice system to collaborate with other sectors so as to address the root causes of disputes and avert violence, conflict, and human rights abuses.

Effective prevention strategies should have three objectives in view: first, to promote trust in justice systems. They must provide people with a reasonable expectation that their rights will be protected, their disputes managed peacefully, and that they will be safeguarded from abuses of power.

Second, they must tackle the root causes of injustice. They must provide legal identity and other documentation and empower communities and marginalized groups to realize their rights and overcome unfairness. Third, they must use the law to reduce risk. They must strengthen legislative frameworks for the prevention of violence and implement laws and regulations that make it less likely that disputes will arise or escalate.

The Task Force thought that four levers could help national reformers as they work towards justice for all. First, marshalling data and evidence to create awareness of the scale of the problem, while demonstrating how solutions could be cost effective. Second, innovation could bring new players into the justice sector and help develop approaches that could deliver justice at scale.

Third, smarter financing strategies could redirect resources away from ineffective approaches and towards what works. They could also attract finance from other sectors and from non-traditional investors. Fourth, new governance models and shared standards could increase coherence in a justice system, enabling a greater diversity of partners to work together towards a shared result.

When it comes to action at the national level, the Task Force offered three sets of recommendations. First, resolve the justice problems that matter most to people by conducting regular surveys. Second, prevent justice problems and create opportunities for people to participate fully in their societies and economies. Third, invest in justice systems and institutions that work for people and that are equipped to respond to their need for justice.

Such, then, are some of the challenges for judges and lawyers worldwide. And there are others. The International Commission of Jurists, established in 1952, held its triennial Congress in Geneva on Saturday 10 February, 2024. The Congress, which this author attended as an Honorary Commissioner, provided important insights on challenges to democracy and the rule of law worldwide. The insights below are based on the author's notes taken from reports presented to the congress.

Historically, the International Commission of Jurists has developed principles on the rule of law that have been of inestimable value over the years. In 1955, for example, the Commission adopted the 'Act of Athens', which solemnly declared that:

1 The State is subject to the law.
2 The Government should respect the rights of the individual under the Rule of Law and provide effective means for their enforcement.
3 Judges should be guided by the Rule of Law, protect and enforce it without fear or favour, and resist any encroachments by governments or political parties on their independence as judges.
4 Lawyers of the world should preserve the independence of their profession, assert the rights of the individual under the Rule of Law, and insist that every accused is accorded a fair trial.

The ICJ Congress, which was attended by Commissioners, Honorary Commissioners, and representatives of regional sections world-wide, registered that the foregoing principles on democracy and the rule of law are under severe stress in many parts of the world, and are in need of being supplemented and updated in the light of contemporary challenges.

The world, it was pointed out, is changing politically, and the number of undemocratic governments is rising. Leading powers are challenging long-held precepts of human rights – and indeed the very notion that there are universally-valid human rights is under challenge.

Climate change, pandemics, widespread poverty and criminality are challenging the functioning of governments, as well as the administration of justice. And Artificial Intelligence (AI) is presenting opportunities as well as challenges to governance and the administration of justice that are still not well understood. There was an oft-repeated view that one should urgently study the implications of AI for the Rule of Law.

The independence and impartiality of judges, it was reported, have come under attack in many countries. Interference is coming from outside as well as inside the judiciary. Systems for the appointment of judges are slanted in some countries, and, in one instance, the President of the country is Head of the Judicial Council that appoints judges.

Some of the interference with the independence of judges is also coming from inside the judiciary through, for example, high-handedness on the part of Chief Justices in the allocation of cases. In some countries, the judiciary is weaponised and used as an instrument of oppression.

Judges are politically controlled and harassed in many countries. In one country, no one charged has been acquitted over the past ten years. In many countries, disciplinary procedures applicable to judges are opaque and arbitrary. In some countries, standards on the accountability of judges are vague or non-existent.

In some countries, candidates for judicial appointment recommended by judicial commission are not appointed, for political reasons. In some countries, judges are appointed on a contractual basis, meaning that they have to be mindful of the renewal of their contracts. In some instances, where foreign nationals are appointed to judicial positions on a contractual basis, their visas may not be renewed and this can be used as leverage over them.

Problems are acute in countries emerging from conflict – where the standards for appointment and conduct of judges can be quite problematic. The judges in such transitional countries are often in a precarious situation.

In many countries there are prolonged delays in starting trials, and prosecutors press for pre-trial detention without bail. In many countries, women's access to justice faces numerous obstructions, and some judges prefer not to have to deal with cases involving LGBTQI issues. In many countries, the judiciary is not representative of the diversity of the population and in numerous countries men outnumber women on the bench.

The problems affecting democracy and the rule of law in one continent were presented by a rapporteur as follows:

1 A decline of democracy and the rule of law.
2 Corruption in the administration of justice.
3 Organized crime affecting the administration of justice.

4 Scarcity of resources for the administration of justice.
5 Minimal education and training for judges.
6 Inadequate procedures for the selection of judges.
7 Arbitrary disciplinary procedures.
8 Lack of awareness about the ethical use of AI in the administration of justice.

Three important recommendations were offered by this contributor:

1 The International Commission of Jurists should urgently study the issue of political assaults on the judiciary, including from the inside.
2 The International Commission of Jurists should urgently update the international standards on the independence of the judiciary.
3 The International Commission of Jurists should urgently undertake a study on the ethical use of Artificial Intelligence by the judiciary.
4 The available standards on the independence of the judiciary should be widely disseminated, using modern communications technology.

The point was made repeatedly that democracy and the rule of law are under attack in all regions of the world and that the International Commission of Jurists should mobilize to defend them. As it was put by one speaker: "We can no longer take democracy, the rule of law and respect for human rights for granted."

2 A Human Rights Handbook for Judges and Lawyers

There is thus urgent work to be done to safeguard the independence of the judiciary and the role of judges and lawyers. This modest *Human Rights Handbook for Judges and Lawyers* is offered in the belief that national judiciaries have a very important role to play in the protection of human rights in each country, and that it may be useful to judges and lawyers to have, readily available, some foundational insights developed over the years within the international human rights community. Our hope is that this Handbook might be translated into as many local languages as possible and widely distributed.

We start with a discussion of the fundamentals of a National Human Rights Protection System. Every country should have in place an adequate and effective national human rights protection system, and the elements we mention are meant to encourage everyone, including judges and lawyers, to contribute to the enhancement of their country's national human rights protection systems.

We discuss next the human rights obligations of every Member State of the United Nations by virtue of its adherence to the United Nations Charter. The 193 Member States of the United Nations have all undertaken solemn legal commitments to uphold human rights nationally, and to cooperate with the United Nations in its efforts to promote and protect human rights worldwide. Every Government has a duty to abide by its commitments under the Charter. We also present the UN Declaration on Principles of International Law concerning Friendly Relations and Co-operation among States in accordance with the Charter of the United Nations (1970), which is widely considered a codification of the obligations of UN Member States under the Charter. It is important that the judiciary and the legal profession of each country make their contribution to the implementation of the legal obligations of their Governments by virtue of their membership of the United Nations.

We discuss next the legal obligations of States Parties to international human rights treaties, building on General Comment No. 31 of the UN Human Rights Committee, a body functioning under the International Covenant on Civil and Political Rights (1966). This General Comment magisterially summarises the duties and responsibilities of Governments when they ratify a treaty such as the International Covenant.

Next, we present the UN Basic Principles and Guidelines on the Right to a Remedy and Reparation for Victims of Gross Violations of International Human Rights Law and Serious Violations of International Humanitarian Law. These principles and guidelines were meticulously prepared by human rights specialists, notably Professor Theodoor van Boven, Professor of International Law at Maastricht University in the Netherlands, Special Rapporteur of the UN Sub-Commission on Human Rights, scrutinised by the Sub-Commission and the then Commission on Human Rights, and thereafter adopted by the UN General Assembly. It is a set of principles highly pertinent to the work of judges and lawyers.

Thereafter, we introduce the UN Principles on the Independence of the Judiciary. This is a helpful document inasmuch as Judges need to know that, when they carry out their functions, their independence would be respected by everyone concerned. At the triennial Congress of the International Commission of Jurists held on 10 February 2024, there was a widely shared view that the principles are in need of updating in the light of contemporary challenges.

We then offer a discussion of the concept of the universality of human rights and present a Recapitulation of Universally Binding Human Rights Norms: norms that are applicable to every Government in the world as obligations under the UN Charter, peremptory obligations of *jus cogens,* norms of customary international law, or norms corresponding to general principles shared by the principal legal systems of the world.

Thereafter, we proceed to a discussion of the legal content of the responsibilities of Governments to prevent violations of human rights, to 'respect', 'ensure', 'fulfil', 'guarantee', and 'protect' human rights. These are terms that are frequently found in international legal documents on human rights.

We discuss thereafter some legal aspects of the foundational concepts of human dignity, and equality, and continue with a discussion of survival rights such as the right to a safe environment. We draw attention to these foundational concepts and principles because we think that judges and lawyers worldwide would do well to have them in view as they deal with the contemporary challenges of the rule of law in a world in dramatic transformation.

When the then UN Commission on Human Rights began its work at the commencement of the United Nations, its declared objective, in 1947, was to draft and promulgate an International Bill of Rights. The International Bill of Rights remains the indispensable normative framework on human rights for the 193 Member States of the United Nations. We therefore append the International Bill of Rights, which consists of the Universal Declaration of Human Rights (1948), the International Covenant on Civil and Political Rights and its Optional Protocol (1966); and the International Covenant on Economic, Social and Cultural Rights (1966).

We also append a Recapitulation of what we think are universally-binding norms of human rights drawn from the International Bill of Rights and related conventions.

We reproduce the Declaration adopted by the International Commission of Jurists at its triennial Congress in 2019 on the independence of judges and lawyers.

Finally, we refer to a few publications that might be helpful for further reading.

2 The Importance of an Adequate and Effective National Human Rights Protection System in Every Country

1 Introduction

The concept of a national protection system is one of the most strategic for the universal realisation of human rights. The protection of human rights should take place in one's country, where one lives and comes face to face with authority or power. Every country should have in place an adequate and effective national protection system. This is a basic duty of governments, which exist to advance and protect the dignity and rights of their people. This legal duty stems from the obligation of Governments under the UN Charter to uphold human rights within their own countries and to cooperate for the universal promotion and protection of human rights.

It was in this spirit that Article 21 of the Universal Declaration of Human Rights affirmed that the will of the people shall be the basis of the authority of government. This will, shall be expressed in periodic and genuine elections which shall be by universal and equal suffrage and shall be held by secret vote or by equivalent free voting procedures.

Article 25 of the International Covenant on Civil and Political Rights added that everyone shall have the right and the opportunity, without any of the distinctions mentioned in Article 2, and without unreasonable restrictions, (a) to take part in the conduct of public affairs, directly or through freely chosen representatives; (b) to vote and to be elected at genuine periodic elections which shall be by universal and equal suffrage and shall be held by secret ballot, guaranteeing the free expression of the will of the electors; (c) to have access, on general terms of equality, to public service in his or her country.

In this chapter, we shall seek to define the scope of the national responsibility to protect human rights based on the precepts of international law and human rights treaties. We shall begin with some observations on the responsibility to protect, then consider the recommendations of human rights treaty bodies on the need for a national protection system, discuss the dimensions of a national protection system, and then proceed to discuss the implications of international human rights law for a national protection system, the prevention of human rights violations, remedies for human rights violations, the role of the courts, the role of law enforcement agencies, the role of national human rights institutions, the role of human rights education, and the role of national human rights plans of action. These and some additional propositions on the concept of a national protection system will be summarized in the concluding part of the chapter.

2 The National Responsibility to Protect

It is a widely held view in the world today that national, regional, and international activities should be geared towards the respect, realization, and protection of internationally agreed norms of human rights. By human rights are meant all rights, civil and political as well as economic, social and cultural[1]. In the UN Millennium Declaration[2] leaders the world over committed themselves to values for the twenty-first century which give priority to respect for human rights and fundamental freedoms. The Millennium Development Goals[3] sought to halve the number of people living in poverty in the world by 2015 and this aim has now been updated to 2030 by the Sustainable Development Goals.

In a Global Summit held in 2005, world leaders committed themselves to the concept of the responsibility to protect, and pledged to take action against genocide, ethnic cleansing, war crimes, and crimes against humanity. The responsibility to protect, as presented by an independent international commission in December 2001, entails the responsibility to prevent violations of human rights, the responsibility to react and remedy them, and the responsibility to rebuild societies devastated by conflict and gross violations of human rights.

Much attention has been given to the implementation of the responsibility to protect at the international level, but the concept continues to be treated with caution by some countries, particularly developing ones, which fear intervention into their internal affairs by powerful countries. But far less attention has been given to the national responsibility to protect, where the debate needs to be. For it is at home, in each country, that we should seek to build up the protection of human rights.

Whatever debates take place over the international dimensions of the responsibility to protect, there can be no doubt that there is a national responsibility to protect that rests with every Government in the world. This is by virtue of their acceptance of international human rights obligations

---

1 See, the Universal Declaration of Human Rights (1948). International Covenant on Civil and Political Rights (1966); International Covenant on Economic, Social and Cultural Rights (1966).

2 UN General Assembly Resolution 55/2. See, generally, Yash Ghai and Jill Cottrell, *The Millennium Declaration, Rights and Constitutions*. Oxford India, 2011.

3 UN General Assembly Resolution, Millennium Development Goals, 2000.

under the United Nations Charter and international human rights instruments, and their overwhelming affirmations of the universality of human rights in major world gatherings such as the Vienna World Conference on Human Rights, 1993, the Millennium Summit (2000), and the Summit of World Leaders, 2005.

The primary responsibility for the prevention of violations of human rights lies with the national protection system of each State. As has been correctly noted, the first obligation of a Government is to respect and to ensure to all individuals within its territory and subject to its jurisdiction the rights recognized in international human rights treaties.[4] A state complies with the obligation to respect the recognized rights by not violating them. The duty to ensure imposes an affirmative duty on the state and calls for specific activities by the state to enable individuals to enjoy the recognized rights.[5]

The second obligation is for the State to take the necessary steps, in accordance with its constitutional processes, and with the provisions of international human rights treaties it has ratified, to adopt such legislative or other measures as may be necessary to give effect to these rights and freedoms.[6] The third obligation is to ensure that any person whose rights or freedoms are violated shall have an effective remedy, notwithstanding that the violation has been committed by persons acting in an official capacity; to ensure that any person claiming such a remedy shall have his or her right thereto determined by competent judicial, administrative, or legislative authorities, or by the legal system, and to develop the possibilities of judicial review; and to ensure that the competent authorities shall enforce such remedies when granted.[7]

Interpreting Article 13 of the European Convention on Human Rights, which requires that everyone whose rights are violated 'shall have an effective remedy before a national authority', the European Court of Human Rights has observed that the authority referred to may not necessarily be a judicial authority, but, if it is not, its powers and the guarantees which it affords are relevant in determining whether the remedy before it is effective. For a remedy to be 'effective', it is not sufficient that it be provided for by the constitution or by law, or that it be formally recognized; it must be

4 N. Jayawickrama, *The Judicial Application of Human Rights Law: National, Regional and International Jurisprudence.* (2003), p. 46.
5 *Ibid.*, p. 48.
6 *Ibid.*, p. 49.
7 *Ibid.*, p. 49–50.

truly effective in establishing whether there has been a violation of a right and in providing redress.

Human rights treaty bodies have provided significant recommendations on different aspects of the national responsibility to protect human rights that we set out next.

3 The Recommendations of Human Rights Treaty Bodies

Human rights treaty bodies have stressed the importance of the national protection of human rights and of the role that national human rights institutions can play in this process.

3.1 *Implementation at the National Level (General Comment No. 3 (1981) of the Human Rights Committee)*

The Human Rights Committee, in General Comment No. 3 (1981), noted that Article 2 of the International Covenant on Civil and Political Rights (ICCPR) generally left it to the States Parties concerned to choose their method of implementation in their territories within the framework set out in that article. The Committee recognized, in particular, that implementation does not depend solely on constitutional or legislative enactments, which in themselves are not *per se* sufficient. The Committee drew the attention of States Parties to the fact that the obligation under the Covenant is not confined to the respect of human rights, but that States Parties have also undertaken to ensure the enjoyment of these rights to all individuals under their jurisdiction. This aspect called for specific activities by the States Parties to enable individuals to enjoy their rights. In principle this obligation relates to all rights set forth in the Covenant.

In a later General Comment, No. 31 (2004), the Human Rights Committee recalled that Article 2, paragraph 3 of the Covenant required that States Parties make reparation to individuals whose Covenant rights have been violated. Without reparation to individuals whose Covenant rights have been violated, the obligation to provide an effective remedy, which is central to the efficacy of Article 2, paragraph 3, is not discharged. In addition to the explicit reparation required by articles 9, paragraph 5, and Article 14, paragraph 6, the Committee considered that the Covenant, generally, entailed appropriate compensation. The Committee noted that, where appropriate, reparation can involve restitution, rehabilitation and measures of satisfaction, such as public apologies, public memorials, guarantees of non-repetition and changes in relevant laws and practices, as well as bringing to justice the perpetrators of human rights violations.

In general, the purposes of the Covenant would be defeated without an obligation, integral to Article 2, to take measures to prevent the recurrence of a violation of the Covenant. Accordingly, it is a frequent practice of the Committee, in its consideration of individual petitions, to include in its Views the need for measures, beyond a victim-specific remedy, to be taken to avoid recurrence of the type of violation in question. Such measures may require changes in the State Party's laws or practices.

3.2 *Developing a Comprehensive National Strategy (General Comment No. 5 of the Committee on the Rights of the Child)*

In General Comment No. 5 (2003), the Committee on the Rights of the Child dealt with general measures of implementation of the Convention on the Rights of the Child[8]. Included in the General Comment was Part A, "Developing a comprehensive national strategy rooted in the Convention." The Committee pointed out that if Government as a whole, and at all levels, is to promote and respect the rights of the child, it needed to work on the basis of a unifying comprehensive and rights-based national strategy, rooted in the convention.[9] The Committee recommended the development of a comprehensive national strategy or national plan of action for children, built on the framework of the convention. The Committee expected States parties to take account of the recommendations in its concluding observations on their periodic reports when developing and/or reviewing their national strategies. If such a strategy is to be effective, it needed to relate to the situation of all children, and to all the rights in the Convention. It would need to be developed through a process of consultation, including with children and young people and those living and working with them.

To give the strategy authority, it would need to be endorsed at the highest level of government. Also, it needed to be linked to national development planning and included in national budgeting; otherwise, the strategy might remain marginalized outside key decision-making processes. Developing a national strategy was not a one-off task. Once drafted, the strategy would need to be widely disseminated throughout the Government and to the public. The strategy would need to include arrangements for monitoring and continuous review, for regular updating and for periodic reports to parliament and to the public.[10]

---

8 Convention on the Rights of the Child. New York, 1989. 1577 UNTS 3.

9 HRI/GEN/1Rev.9, pp. 428–430.

10 *Ibid.*, p. 429.

3.3 *The Role of National Human Rights Institutions in the Protection of Economic, Social and Cultural Rights (General Comment No. 10 (1998) of the Committee on Economic, Social and Cultural Rights (CESCOR)*

The Committee on Economic, Social and Cultural Rights (CESCOR), in its General Comment No. 10, adopted on 3 December 1998, considered it essential that national human rights institutions give full attention to economic, social and cultural rights in all of the relevant activities of these institutions. It drew up the following indicative list of the types of activities that could be, and in some instances already had been, undertaken by national institutions in relation to these rights:

- The promotion of educational and informational programmes designed to enhance awareness and understanding of economic, social and cultural rights both within the population at large and among particular groups such as the public service, the judiciary, the private sector and the labour movement;
- The scrutinizing of existing laws and administrative acts as well as draft bills and other proposals to ensure that they are consistent with the requirements of the International Covenant on Economic, Social and Cultural Rights,
- Providing technical advice, or undertaking surveys in relation to economic, social and cultural rights, including when requested by the public authorities or other appropriate agencies;
- The identification of national level benchmarks against which the realization of Covenant obligations can be measured;
- Conducting research and inquiries designed to ascertain the extent to which particular economic, social and cultural rights are being realized, either within the State as a whole or in relation to communities of particular vulnerability,
- Examining complaints alleging violations of applicable economic, social and cultural rights standards within the State.

The Committee called upon States Parties to ensure that the mandates accorded to all national human rights institutions include appropriate attention to economic, social and cultural rights and requested States Parties to include details both of the mandates and the principal relevant activities of such institutions in their reports submitted to the Committee.

3.4 *CERD General Recommendation XVII (1993) on the Establishment of National Institutions to Facilitate the Implementation of the Convention*

The Committee on the Elimination of Racial Discrimination (CERD), convinced of the need to encourage further the establishment of national institutions to facilitate the implementation of the Convention, recommended that States Parties establish national commissions or other appropriate bodies, taking into account the Paris Principles, to serve, *inter alia,* the following purposes:

- To promote respect for the enjoyment of human rights without any discrimination, as expressly set out in article 5 of the ICERD;
- To review government policy on protection against racial discrimination;
- To monitor legislative compliance with the provisions of the Convention;
- To educate the public about the obligations of States Parties under the Convention;
- To assist the Government in the preparation of reports submitted to the Committee.

CERD further recommended that, where such commissions had already been established, they should be associated with the preparation of reports and possibly included in government delegations in order to intensify the dialogue between the Committee and the State Party concerned.

3.5 *CEDAW General Recommendation 6 (1988) on Effective National Machinery and Publicity*

The Committee on the Elimination of Discrimination Against Women (CEDAW) has recommended that States Parties establish and/or strengthen effective national machinery, institutions and procedures, at a high level of Government, and with adequate resources, commitment and authority to:

- Advise on the impact on women of all government policies;
- Monitor the situation of women comprehensively;
- Help formulate new policies and effectively carry out strategies and measures to eliminate discrimination;
- Take appropriate steps to ensure the dissemination of the Convention, the reports of the States Parties under article 18 and the reports of the Committee in the language of the States concerned.

3.6 *Other Treaty Bodies*

Other treaty bodies have made detailed recommendations for national preventive and protective arrangements, particularly for the prevention of genocide and torture. The foregoing recommendations of human rights treaty bodies were tailored to the requirements of their respective treaty. It is necessary to go beyond them and to consider more comprehensively the concept of a national protection system, which we do in the following section.

4 The Concept of a National Protection System

A national protection system has the following key dimensions that we shall discuss below: constitutional, legislative, judicial, institutional, educational, and preventive. In addition, it requires an independent and efficient judiciary and law enforcement systems, and human rights education. National human rights plans of action can also help reinforce a national protection system.

4.1 *Constitutional Dimension*

The constitutional structure of a country is a matter for the sovereign choice of its people. However, three issues require particular attention and scrutiny from the perspectives of international human rights law: first its fundamental human rights guarantees; second, its judicial institutions; and third, its national institutions for the protection of human rights.

Fundamental human rights guarantees in the Constitution or the Bill of Rights, if there is one, should not be less but may be more than what is provided for in international human rights law. Each country should be able to show that it has done two things: first, that it has methodically made a comparison between the provisions of its fundamental human rights guarantees and those in the principal international human rights instruments; second that rights guaranteed in international customary law, particularly norms of *jus cogens*, are among its constitutional human rights guarantees.

The Second Restatement of the Foreign Relations Laws of the USA provides a good summary of rights that are guaranteed in international law:

"A state is obliged to respect the human rights of persons subject to its jurisdiction that it has (a) undertaken to respect by international agreements;(b) that states generally are bound to respect as a matter of customary international law; and (c) that it is required to respect under general principles of law common to the major legal systems of the world"[11]

"A state violates international customary law if, as a matter of state policy, it practices, encourages, or condones:

- Genocide.
- Slavery or slave trade.
- The murder or causing the disappearance of individuals
- Torture or other cruel, inhuman or degrading treatment or punishment.
- Prolonged arbitrary detention
- Systematic racial discrimination, or

---

11 Article 701.

- A consistent pattern of gross violations of internationally recognized human rights."[12]

4.2 *Legislative Dimension*

International law gives a discretion to States whether they would make treaties they have accepted to be bound by directly applicable in their legal systems, or whether they would reflect the provisions of those treaties in national legislation. Whichever route a country chooses, there is an obligation to make sure that its national laws correspond to its legal commitments under international human rights law or international human rights treaties. National parliaments should exercise oversight over whether this obligation has been met and, where action is required, see to it that legislative changes or enactments are done. The human rights treaty bodies operating under particular international conventions often make suggestions for legislative updating, and national parliaments should require regular reports from the Executive about the recommendations of the human rights treaty bodies. There is a role for parliamentary oversight over Governmental compliance with international human rights obligations. Each parliament should ideally establish a human rights committee to perform this role.

4.3 *Judicial Dimension*

The judicial dimension requires that courts be independent and effective. There are United Nations declarations and statements on the meaning of judicial independence and effectiveness, which we shall discuss later in this book. As already indicated, international law leaves it to the choice of a Government whether it makes a treaty directly applicable in its legal system or whether it enacts legislation incorporating the obligations under the treaty. It would be our submission, however, that international human rights norms of *jus cogens* status, and human rights norms that have the status of international customary law should be directly applicable in national courts.

International law makes it obligatory that each State provide adequate guarantees against human rights violations. This responsibility falls, in the first place, primarily upon the national judiciary. In the event that there is a failure to protect, there may be remedies under international law. The Second American Restatement, which we cited earlier, summarized these remedies as follows:

"(1) A state party to an international human rights agreement has, as

---

12 Article 702.

against any other state party violating the agreement, the remedies generally available for violation of an international agreement, as well as any special remedies provided by the agreement;

"(2) Any state may pursue international remedies against any other state for a violation of the customary international law of human rights.

"(3) An individual victim of a violation of human rights agreement may pursue any remedy provided by that agreement or by other applicable international agreements."[13]

It is of great importance that judges and legal practitioners be provided with access to the key decisions of international human rights bodies in local languages so that they may be aware of them and may draw upon them. This is a task on which international human rights organizations and NGOs may assist. But it would be important also that national ministries of justice, or their equivalent, pay attention to this matter so that judges may have access to the latest human rights precedents and reasoning.

4.4 *Institutional Dimension*

Experience has shown that, in addition to the courts, institutions such as national human rights commissions, national human rights commissioners or ombudspersons can be quite helpful in advancing and protecting human rights.[14] International law does not make such institutions mandatory but, as a matter of policy, a country should periodically assess its institutional arrangements, or lack thereof to see whether the establishment of national human rights bodies could be helpful for the protection of human rights.

The Paris Principles provide that national human rights institutions could perform, among others, key tasks such as: seeking an amicable settlement of human rights grievances through conciliation, binding decision or other means; informing the complainant of his or her rights and of available means of redress, and promoting access to such redress; hearing complaints or referring them to a competent authority; and making recommendations to the competent authorities, including proposals for amendment of laws, regulations, or administrative practices that obstruct the free exercise of rights.

---

13 Article 703.

14 See, generally, B.G. Ramcharan (Ed.), *The Protection Roles of National Human Rights Institutions*. Martinus Nijhoff, Leiden, 2005. J.A. Mertus, *Human Rights Matters. Local Politics and National Human Rights Institutions*. Stanford, Stanford University Press, 2009.

4.5 *Monitoring Dimension*

The responsibility to protect and to prevent violations of human rights demands that every country monitor itself to detect situations of distress and to address them well before they erupt into violations of human rights or conflict.[15] This calls for independent bodies that will systematically watch out for such distress situations and draw attention to them. A national human rights commission could be given the mandate to do this. In multi-ethnic countries special arrangements may need to be devised. But the concept of self-monitoring is a vital part of a national protection system.

A national protection system should provide for adequate and effective remedies to prevent violations of human rights and to provide redress in cases of breach. The absence of a remedy available to test an arguable claim for breach amounts to a violation of human rights [16] The right to an effective remedy may, in certain circumstances, require Governments to provide for, and implement, provisional or interim measures to avoid continuing violations and to endeavour to repair at the earliest possible opportunity any harm that may have been done.[17]

A national protection system should be particularly attentive to the risks of genocide, ethnic cleansing, crimes against humanity and war crimes and should provide effective guarantees against them. As the Human Rights Committee stated in its General Comment 6/16 of 27 July 1982, States have the supreme duty to prevent wars, acts of genocide, and other acts of mass violence causing arbitrary loss of life. A national protection system should provide for a system of regular visits by national, regional or international bodies to all places of detention.

In the event of a violation of human rights, the national protection system must provide for measures, beyond a victim-specific remedy, to be taken to avoid recurrence of the type of violation in question. Such measures may require changes in the State's laws or practices.[18]

A national protection system should provide for investigations of gross violations of human rights and for justice to the victims. A national protection system should provide for safeguards against deportation or extradition to a state where the deportee/extraditee may face serious risks of torture or arbitrary execution. A national protection system should be particularly protective of human rights defenders. A national human rights

15 See, generally, B.G. Ramcharan, *Preventive Human Rights Strategies in a World of New Threats and Challenges*. London, Routledge, 2009.

16 See the Annual Report of the Human Rights Committee, 2001, *Faure v. Australia.*

17 See General Comment 31 of the Human Rights Committee.

18 See General Comment 31 of the Human Rights Committee.

system should give priority to the prevention of violations of human rights, to which we turn next.

5 The Prevention of Human Rights Violations

The national responsibility to protect entails prevention, reaction, remedies, and measures to prevent recurrence. National legal systems provide for preventive measures such as judicial review, quashing orders (certiorari), mandatory orders (mandamus), prohibiting orders (prohibition), Habeas corpus, and statutory mechanisms of challenge, including injunctions.[19] Section 6 of the Hong Kong Bill of Rights, for example, provided at one stage that a court or tribunal might grant such remedy or relief in respect of such a breach, violation, *or threatened violation* as it has power to make or grant and as it considers appropriate and just in the circumstances.

The national responsibility to protect requires that Governments fulfil their obligations under international human rights treaties with preventive requirements such as: the Convention on the Prevention and Punishment of Genocide; the Convention against Torture; the Optional Protocol to the Convention against Torture (OPCAT),[20] which provides for regular visits by national bodies and by the Subcommittee for the Prevention of Torture to prisons and places of detention. There are also preventive obligations under other international human rights norms and jurisprudence that we discuss next.

5.1 *Preventive Protection of the Right to Life*

Article 6 of the International Covenant on Civil and Political Rights (1966) protects the right to life, which the Human Rights Committee, the monitoring body established under the Covenant, has deemed 'the supreme right from which no derogation is permitted even in time of public emergency which threatens the life of the nation (article 4)'.[21] The Committee considers that

> States have the supreme duty to prevent wars, acts of genocide and

---

19 See, e.g. Clive Lewis, *Judicial Remedies in Public Law*. London, Sweet and Maxwell (2008).

20 The European Convention for the Prevention of Torture also provides for a system of visits.

21 General Comment 6/16 of 27 July, 1982. Reproduced in M. Nowak, *The International Covenant on Civil and Political Rights. A Commentary*, Engel Publishers, 2006, p. 1092.

> other acts of mass violence causing arbitrary loss of life. Every effort they make to avert the danger of war, especially thermo-nuclear war, and to strengthen international peace and security would constitute the most important condition and guarantee for the safeguarding of the right to life. In this respect the Committee noted, in particular, a connection between article 6 and article 20, which states that the law shall prohibit any propaganda for war or incitement to violence.[22]

The Committee continued:

> The protection against arbitrary deprivation of life which is explicitly required by the third sentence of article 6(1) is of paramount importance. The Committee considers that States parties should take measures not only to prevent and punish deprivation of life by criminal acts, but also to prevent arbitrary killing by their own security forces. The deprivation of life by the authorities of the State is a matter of the utmost gravity. Therefore, the law must strictly control and limit the circumstances in which a person may be deprived of his life by such authorities.
>
> States parties should also take specific and effective measures to prevent the disappearance of individuals, something which unfortunately has become all too frequent and leads too often to arbitrary deprivation of life. Furthermore, States should establish effective facilities and procedures to investigate thoroughly cases of missing and disappeared persons in circumstances which may involve a violation of the right to life.[23]

5.2 *Preventive Dimensions of the Right to an Effective Remedy*

Professor Manfred Nowak has noted that whether a remedy is effective may ultimately be determined only on the basis of concrete cases, taking into consideration all relevant circumstances. In some cases, the formal chain of judicial appeals is the only possible effective protection; in others, informal, preventive measures (e.g., against the application of torture or against arbitrary executions) may be much more effective than a subsequent determination by a constitutional court. On the other hand, when judicial case law functions well and is adhered to by administrative organs, it

22 General Comment 6/16 of 27 July, 1982. Reproduced in M. Nowak, *The International Covenant on Civil and Political Rights. A Commentary*, Engel Publishers, 2006, p. 1092.

23 *Ibid.*

may in the long term be far more effective in preventing similar violations in the future than, e.g. large-scale efforts to train civil servants.[24]

Does the right to an effective remedy, ensured by Art. 2, refer, as suggested by the formulation of para. 3(a), only to a repressive remedy after violation of a substantive right has occurred, or are States parties also required to take preventive measures? The Human Rights Committee dealt extensively with this problem in *C.F. et al v. Canada* (No. 113/198). In implementing Article 25 of the Covenant, the Quebec Election Act had been amended in 1979 to recognize the right of inmates to vote. However, the implementation of the specific voting procedures was made subject to an administrative agreement, which the Solicitor General initially refused to sign for federal inmates. As a result, three inmates filed a request for a temporary injunction with the Federal court of first instance to force the Solicitor-General to conclude the administrative agreement in time for the provincial elections, but this was denied.

The issue subsequently came before the Human Rights Committee. On the issue whether Article 2 afforded preventive remedies and whether a declaratory judgment in favour of the authors following the election would have been an effective remedy within the meaning of Article 2(3) of the Covenant and Art. 5(2) of the Optional Protocol, the Committee stated:

> With respect to Article 5, Paragraph 2(b) of the Optional Protocol the Committee observed that, although the authors might not have been able to obtain a declaratory judgment before the elections of 13 April, 1981, a subsequent judgment could nevertheless in principle have been an effective remedy in the meaning contemplated by Article 2, Paragraph 3 of the Covenant and Article 5, Paragraph 2(b) of the Optional Protocol. The Covenant provides that a remedy shall be granted whenever a violation of one of the rights guaranteed by it has occurred; consequently, it does not generally prescribe preventive protection, but confines itself to requiring effective redress ex post facto.[25]

Professor Nowak commented critically on this finding:

> In other words, the Committee reached the problematic conclusion from Article 2(3)(a) that this provision is limited to *repressive remedies* and 'generally' does not require preventive protection. ...The reasoning behind this decision is so unjustifiably broad as to miss the

24 Nowak, *op. cit.*, p. 65.
25 *C.F. et al. v. Canada* (No. 113/1981).

> purpose of providing individuals with effective remedies. Would the Committee have decided differently if – instead of the right to vote – a deportation, the right to personal liberty, the prohibition of torture or even the right to life had been affected?...[26]

Nowak noted, however, that following its General Comment on the right to life, the Committee subsequently made it known in *Herrera Rubio v. Colombia* that as regards this right, Article 2 also required preventive measures, such as deterring the disappearance of persons.

It may also be recalled that in its General Comment 31, the Committee stated the following:

> The right to an effective remedy may in certain circumstances require States Parties to provide for and implement provisional or interim measures to avoid continuing violations and to endeavour to repair at the earliest possible opportunity any harm that may have been caused by such violations.[27]

5.3 *Interim Measures of Protection*

Interim measures of protection are a valuable method of preventive protection practiced by international judicial and human rights bodies, including the International Court of Justice, the European Court of Human Rights, the Inter-American Court of Human Rights, the African Commission on Human and Peoples' Rights, the UN Human Rights Committee, the United Nations Committee against Torture, and the Inter-American Commission on Human Rights. In the words of one scholar:

> An author of interim measures may require that the State take positive action, such as providing protection for human rights activists or journalists, or it may call upon the State to refrain from taking action, such as not extraditing a person or delaying the execution of prisoners until their cases have been resolved before the international body. The purpose of interim measures in international human rights law is most often to protect the persons involved in a case from urgent danger of grave and irreparable injury.[28]

---

26 Nowak, *op. cit.*, p. 65ff.

27 Human Rights Committee, General Comment No. 31.

28 J.M. Pasqualucci, "Interim Measure in International Human Rights: Evolution and Harmonization", *Vanderbilt Journal of International Law*, January, 2005.

The author continued that, in general, many States have accepted the decisions of international courts that interim measures are binding on the States that are parties to the applicable treaties. However, some States have not. The author contended that interim measures are implied in the constituent documents that provide the right of individual petition and must be considered to be binding on States that are parties.[29]

5.4 *Deportation and Extradition to Countries Where There is Risk of Serious Violation of Human Rights: Preventive Protection*

The jurisprudence of international and regional human rights bodies provides for preventive protection in the event that a potential deportee/extraditee would be liable to suffer inhuman treatment, for example political persecution in the country to which they are to be sent, or the death penalty.[30] In the Soering case, decided by the European Court of Human Rights, Jens Soering, a German national, was 18 when he and his girl-friend were alleged to have killed her parents in Virginia, USA. Soering was subsequently arrested in England and his extradition was sought to the United States. The State of Virginia had the death penalty for murder, and it was usual for prisoners to spend between six and eight years on death row before being executed. Were he to be extradited, Soering might face the death penalty and the death row phenomenon. An extradition order obtained in the English courts was put into suspense pending determination of Soering's application to the then European Commission on Human Rights. The case eventually reached the European Court of Human Rights, which apparently took into consideration that Soering could have been extradited to Germany, his country of nationality. The Court held:

> (H)aving regard to the very long period of time spent on death row in such extreme conditions, with the ever present and mounting anguish of awaiting execution of the death penalty, and to the personal circumstances of the applicant, especially his age and mental state at the time of the offence, the applicant's extradition to the United States would expose him to a real risk of treatment going beyond the threshold set by Article 3. A further consideration of relevance is that in the particular instance the legitimate purpose of extradition could

---

29 *Ibid.*

30 See F. Jacobs, *et al.*, *The European Convention on Human Rights*, Fourth Edition, Oxford, Oxford University Press, 2006, p. 101.

> be achieved by another means which would not involve suffering of such exceptional intensity or duration.[31]

The Court therefore held that the UK Secretary of State's decision to extradite Soering to the United States would, if implemented, give rise to a breach of Article 3 of the European Convention on Human Rights.

With regard to prevention strategies in the future, it would be advisable that every country, once every five years or so, commission an analysis of threats of gross violations of human rights with a view to taking preventive action. Such an analysis could be done by the national human rights commission, where it exists. National human rights commissions in existence should include a threat assessment in their annual reports. Poverty alleviation strategies should, in the future, be built on preventive approaches, with the accent being on preventing poverty where this could be done using existing resources within a country. At the end of the day, this is a task of efficient governance.

With new threats and challenges facing the world, national prevention systems should also have in view the human rights dimensions of issues such as: Climate change; Water shortage; Pandemics; Mass migration; and Artificial Intelligence. It is also important for national prevention systems to be vigilant in respect of: violence against women, trafficking in human beings; breaches of human rights and humanitarian law during armed conflicts; gross violations of human rights.[32]

5.5 *Remedies for Human Rights Violations*

The World Conference on Human Rights (1993) expressed grave concern about continuing human rights violations in all parts of the world, in disregard of standards contained in international human rights instruments and international humanitarian law, and about the lack of sufficient and effective remedies for the victims."[33] This situation, unfortunately, has not changed.

Remedies for violations of human rights may be found in the areas of constitutional law, public law, criminal law and the law of torts. The constitution may provide for remedies for breach and, in Commonwealth jurisdictions, the courts will review an exercise of power to ensure that a public body has not made an error of law; has considered all relevant factors,

---

31 See F. Jacobs, *et al.*, *The European Convention on Human Rights*, *op. cit.*, p. 103.

32 See, generally, B.G. Ramcharan, *Preventive Human Rights Strategies. Strategies in a World of Acute Threats and Challenges.* Routledge, 2010.

33 Vienna Declaration (1993), para. 29.

and not taken into account any irrelevant factors; has acted for a purpose expressly or impliedly authorized by statute; has not acted in a way that is so unreasonable that no reasonable public body would act in that way; and that the public body has observed statutory procedural requirements and the common law principles of natural justice or procedural fairness. These grounds were summarized by Lord Diplock as illegality, irrationality, and procedural impropriety.[34]

As indicated earlier, judicial review may take the form of a quashing order, a mandatory order, a prohibiting order, a declaration or injunction, damages, restitution, or recovery of money. The prerogative writ of habeas corpus is still available in Commonwealth countries as a means of challenging the legality of the detention of an individual by a public body. Furthermore, Statute may provide a means by which the legality of decisions of public bodies may be challenged in the courts.[35] There may also be remedies in tort for human rights abuses.[36]

6 The Role of the Courts and of Law Enforcement Agencies

We have already alluded to the foundational importance of the role of the courts and of law enforcement agencies. In this section we shall touch on the essentiality of these institutions upholding and conforming to international human rights standards. The Basic Principles on the Independence of the Judiciary, endorsed by the United Nations General Assembly on 13 December, 1985,[37] called for the independence of the judiciary to be guaranteed by the State and enshrined in the Constitution or law of the country. It is the duty of governmental and other institutions to respect and observe the independence of the judiciary. The judiciary, for its part, shall decide matters before them impartially, on the basis of the facts and in accordance with the law, without any restrictions, improper influences, inducements, pressures, threats or interferences, direct or indirect, from any quarter or for any reason.

The judiciary shall have jurisdiction over all issues of a judicial nature and shall have exclusive authority to decide whether an issue submitted for its decision is within its competence as defined by law. There shall not be any inappropriate or unwarranted interference with the judicial process,

---

34 See Clive Lewis, *Judicial Remedies in Public Law*. London, Sweet and Maxwell, 2008.

35 *Ibid.*

36 See on this, G.P. Fletcher, *Tort Liability for Human Rights Abuses*. Oxford, Hart Publishing, 2008.

37 UN General Assembly Resolution 40/32.

nor shall judicial decisions by the courts be subject to revision. Everyone shall have the right to be tried by ordinary courts or tribunals using established legal procedures. Tribunals that do not use the duly established procedures of the legal process shall not be created to displace the jurisdiction belonging to the ordinary courts of judicial tribunals.

The principle of the independence of the judiciary entitles and requires the judiciary to ensure that judicial proceedings are conducted fairly and that the rights of the parties are respected. It is the duty of each Government to provide adequate resources to enable the judiciary to properly perform its functions.

The Code of Conduct for Law Enforcement Officials adopted by the UN General Assembly on 17 December, 1979[38] states that law enforcement officials shall at all times fulfil the duty imposed upon them by law, by serving the community and by protecting all persons against illegal acts, consistent with the high degree of responsibility required by their profession. In the performance of their duty, they shall respect and protect human rights and maintain and uphold the human rights of all persons. They may use force only when strictly necessary and to the extent required for the performance of their duty. Matters of a confidential nature in the possession of law enforcement officials shall be kept confidential, unless the performance of duty or the needs of justice strictly require otherwise.

No law enforcement official may inflict, instigate or tolerate any act of torture or other cruel, inhuman or degrading treatment or punishment, nor may any law enforcement official invoke superior orders or exceptional circumstances such as a state of war or a threat of war, a threat to national security, internal political instability or any other pubic emergency as a justification of torture or other cruel, inhuman or degrading treatment or punishment.

Law enforcement officials shall ensure the full protection of the health of persons in their custody and, in particular, shall take immediate action to secure medical attention whenever required. Law enforcement officials shall not commit any act of corruption. They shall also rigorously oppose and combat all such acts. Law enforcement officials shall respect the law and the principles in the Code of Conduct. They shall also, to the best of their ability, prevent and rigorously oppose any violations of them. Law enforcement officials who have reasons to believe that a violation of the Code has occurred, or is about to occur, shall report the matter to their superior authorities and, where necessary, to other appropriate authorities or organs vested with reviewing or remedial power.

38 UN General Assembly Resolution 34/169.

It is sad to admit that the Basic Principles on the Independence of the Judiciary and the Code of Conduct for Law Enforcement Officials are violated in numerous countries. That, however, does not diminish their validity, and it is precisely the challenge of all national protection systems to strive to live up to them.

7 The Role of National Human Rights Institutions

Even before the adoption of the Universal Declaration of Human Rights, the UN Economic and Social Council, in 1946, recognized that national implementation arrangements and human rights information and education would be essential to take forward the task of implementing the provisions of the Declaration universally. The Council invited Member States to consider the desirability of establishing information groups or local human rights committees to collaborate with them in furthering the work of the UN Commission on Human Rights. The former Commission on Human Rights, early on, highlighted these two aspects and decided to give them particular attention.

The attention given to both subjects, however, would be spasmodic in subsequent years. The Commission did call for reports from the UN Secretariat on the topic and also mandated the holding of world-wide seminars on the role of national institutions in the promotion and protection of human rights. A UN Seminar on National Institutions for the Promotion and Protection of Human Rights, held in 1978, put forward a set of helpful guidelines for the functioning of national human rights institutions. Those guidelines were further built upon in the Principles relating to the Status of National Institutions (The Paris Principles), which were endorsed by the General Assembly in its Resolution 48/134 of 20 December, 1993.

The Paris Principles called for national institutions to have responsibilities such as: submitting recommendations, proposals and reports on matters relating to human rights to the Government, Parliament, or other competent bodies; promoting conformity of national laws and practices with international human rights standards; encouraging ratification and implementation of international standards; contributing to the reporting procedure under international instruments; assisting in formulating and executing human rights teaching and research programmes and increasing public awareness of human rights through information and education; and cooperating with the United Nations, regional institutions and national institutions of other countries.

In 2003, the then High Commissioner for Human Rights wrote to all Governments inviting them to provide concise summaries of their national protection systems under the following headings: 1. In what ways are the provisions of the principal human rights instruments and treaties reflected in the constitution of the country? 2 Is there an oversight process on the reflection of international human rights norms in national legislation? 3. What is the experience of the judiciary in drawing upon the provisions of international human rights norms when considering cases before them? 4. Are there any specific arrangements to promote human rights education in the country? 5. What specialized national human rights institutions are in existence and which of their good practices can be highlighted? 6. Are there arrangements to detect and anticipate threats to human rights of groups at risk?

A report that the Office of High Commissioner submitted to the Commission in 2004 summarized the replies of some three dozen countries. It showed that each country had positive experiences to report but that few of them had previously thought methodically about the six questions in their policy and governmental frameworks. The aim of the exercise was precisely to encourage each country to consider the six questions as a policy framework and, eventually, to publish a world report on the national protection systems of each country.[39]

As part of his reform programme, and as suggested by the Office of High Commissioner, former UN Secretary-General Kofi Annan had called on the different parts of the United Nations system to concert their endeavours to support the efforts of Governments to develop, or enhance, their national protection systems. Pursuant to this decision, a programme of cooperation was worked out to help support the enhancement of national protection systems. The aim of the process was two-fold: to respond positively to requests by Governments for support in strengthening their national protection systems; and to follow the recommendations of the human rights treaty bodies and the human rights special procedures with a view to seeing discreetly in what areas a government might be in need of assistance. A national protection system, as advanced by the Office of High Commissioner and by the Secretary-General, has six dimensions that we discussed earlier in this chapter.

National human rights institutions are an essential component of a national protection system. Each National Commission could map and analyze the human rights history of the country and the contemporary and fu-

39 UN doc. E/CN.4/2004/12/Add. 1: Progress report on support for the strengthening of national human rights protection systems. See, generally, B.G. Ramcharan (Ed.), *The Protection Roles of National Human Rights Institutions.* Martinus Nijhoff, Leiden, 2005.

ture challenges of protection. Each National Commission could do a study on the state of economic, social and cultural rights and identify issues and situations of concern. National Commissions could do a study of situations where there is evidence of a consistent pattern of gross violations of human rights. National Commissions could do a study of population groups at risk. National Commissions could offer policy recommendations for the advancement of women's rights. National Commissions could maintain, as a principal focus, policies and strategies for the prevention of gross violations of human rights. National Commissions could encourage and support the work of judges in the protection of human rights. National Commissions could disseminate the core international human rights norms and jurisprudence to judges and magistrates. National Commissions could develop a policy for the spread of human rights education in schools and higher institutions of learning. National Commissions could enhance their cooperation with protection partners.

The Ninth International Conference of National Institutions for the Promotion and Protection of Human Rights held in Nairobi from 21–24 October, 2009, adopted the Nairobi Declaration in which they underlined that the State has the primary responsibility to protect, promote and respect human rights and ensure that the administration of justice is in full compliance with both international and domestic obligations. They felt that National Institutions could support Governments in the application of international standards and follow-up.

They further considered that the rule of law and administration of justice were of fundamental importance and saw an important role for the judiciary in applying human rights norms and in the development of a strong national system for human rights protection. They thought that National Institutions could help in ensuring an effective administration of justice, in particular with regard to access to justice. The rule of law should be based on a Constitution and national legislation, consistent with international standards and principles.

They considered that NHRIs should play an oversight role over law enforcement agencies and seek to protect the rights of prisoners and detainees. They felt that National institutions should monitor their Government's obligation to respect, protect and fulfil the rights of all people in detention, especially vulnerable or marginalized groups, and support their reintegration within society. NHRIs should also strive to strengthen the correctional system and its personnel. They supported the role of NHRIs in receiving cases of human rights violations and assisting victims. They also supported the role of NHRIs in seeking informal legal redress mechanisms through conciliation or through binding decisions.

They saw for themselves a role in publicizing the findings of treaty bodies and human rights rapporteurs of the UN Human Rights Council. They also saw a role in promoting incorporation of international norms into national law. Furthermore, they saw a role in providing recommendations to strengthen the legal system and judiciary and in promoting adherence and compliance of the judiciary with international human rights norms, including through amicus briefs and legal education. They thought they could help in encouraging and supporting the establishment of legal aid centres.

They saw a preventive role for national human rights institutions, which we discuss next.

8 The Preventive Role of National Human Rights Institutions

For the most part, national human rights institutions remain fledgling institutions, especially in developing countries. Their protection role is still largely undeveloped.[40] Their explicit prevention role is even thinner. However, as with all human rights activities, one can always claim that promotional work is meant to serve the cause of prevention, in the here and now and in the future.

One can say that national human rights institutions nowadays contribute to prevention in one or more of the following ways:

- Undertaking surveys and studies of issues and making recommendations on them.
- Drawing attention to problems in their annual reports or in periodic statements they might issue.
- Undertaking historical analysis of the experience of a country with regard to human rights and drawing lessons from the analysis.
- Undertaking visits to prisons and places of detention.
- Calling for the enactment of laws to correct problems in the society.
- Engaging in good offices activities with governments and law enforcement agencies.

However, much more preventive work is required inside all countries. National institutions should undertake regular risk analysis from the perspectives of human rights. The following checklist of issues could be kept in mind when undertaking risk assessment through human rights lens:

40 See on this, B.G. Ramcharan (Ed.), *The Protection Roles of National Human Rights Institutions*. Martinus Nijhoff, Leiden, 2005.

(a) What is the ethnic composition of the country? Is there a minority population? Is there an indigenous population? Is there a migrant population?
(b) Is there a unifying vision of the country?
(c) What is the state of governance? Is there a functioning democracy?
(d) What is the state of the rule of law and the courts?
(e) Is there an effective national protecting system?
(f) Are there major grievances within the population?
(g) Is there an internal system of early warming and alert to head off grievances?
(h) Is there a *de jure* or *de facto* state of emergency?
(i) Are there gross violations of human rights?
(j) What is the state of human rights of women?
(k) Is there a problem of human trafficking in the country?
(l) What is the state of respect for the rights of the child?
(m) What is the state of the freedoms of expression, religion or belief?
(n) What is the national security doctrine of the state?
(o) What are the UN human rights treaty bodies and the UN human rights investigations reporting about the country?
(p) What are the leading international human rights organizations reporting about the country?
(q) Are there reputable human rights NGOs in the country and what are they reporting?
(r) Are perpetrators of gross violations of human rights being brought to justice?

9 Conclusion

Whatever activities are undertaken at the international or the regional level on behalf of the promotion and the protection of human rights, it is of the utmost importance that every country strive for an adequate and effective national human rights protection system. Judges and lawyers are at the heart of the protection system of every country. In this chapter, we have adduced some considerations that they might keep in mind as they seek to contribute to the establishment or maintenance of adequate and effective national national human rights protection systems.

3 The Legal Obligations of Governments under the UN Charter and the International Bill of Rights

1 Introduction

According to the very first article of the United Nations Charter, the Purposes of the United Nations are, among others, to achieve international cooperation in solving international problems of an economic, social cultural or humanitarian character and in promoting and encouraging respect for human rights and for fundamental freedoms for all without distinction as to race, language, sex, or religion, and to be a centre for harmonizing the actions of nations in the attainment of these common ends. Article 55 of the Charter gives the United Nations a mandate to promote universal respect for, and observance of, human rights and fundamental freedoms for all. In Article 56, all Members of the UN pledged themselves to take joint and separate action in cooperation with the Organization for the achievement of the purposes set forth in Article 55.

Goodrich, Hambro and Simons, in their historic commentary on the Charter, noted that the United Nations was not intended to have the powers of a government; rather, its function was conceived as that of serving as a means of promoting cooperation between States in finding solutions to common problems and of achieving maximum support from members for the work of the Organization.[1]

On the legal thrust of Article 56 of the Charter, Goodrich, Hambro and Simons pointed out, as regards the phrase "in cooperation with the Organization", that while it did not mean that recommendations of UN organs become binding, it did mean "that members are obligated to refrain from obstructionist tactics and to cooperate in good faith to achieve the goals specified in Article 55."[2]

The more recent commentary on the Charter of the United Nations, edited by Bruno Simma (later a judge on the International Court of Justice), noted that, as far as the protection of human rights is concerned, Article 1(3) had been invoked with respect to the improvement generally within the United Nations system of the effective enjoyment of human rights and

1 L. Goodrich, E. Hambro and A. Simons, *Charter of the United Nations: Commentary and Documents*, (New York, London: Columbia University Press, 1969), p. 35.

2 L. Goodrich, E. Hambro and A. Simons, *Charter of the United Nations: Commentary and Documents*, Third Ed. (New York, London: Columbia University Press, 1969), p. 381.

fundamental freedoms and with respect to particular human rights issues and situations.[3]

The same commentary concluded that Article 56 represented a specification of the obligations of member states set forth in Article 2(2) and Article 55. This specification dealt with the three elements of Article 56: joint action, separate action, and cooperation with the organisation in respect of the obligations assumed under Article 55. R. Wolfrum, the author of the Commentary on Article 56 in this volume, agreed with Goodrich, Hambro and Simons, that Article 56 did "require that member states cooperate with the UN in a constructive way; obstructive policies are thus excluded".[4]

The obligations of Member States under the UN Charter were clarified in a famous Declaration adopted on the twenty-fifth anniversary of the United Nations, which we outline next.

2 The UN Declaration on Principles of International Law

In Resolution 2625 (XXV) of 24 October 1970, the UN General Assembly adopted the Declaration on Principles of International Law Concerning Friendly Relations and Cooperation Among States in accordance with the Charter of the United Nations. This declaration is considered a codification of the legal principles of the United Nations Charter. In the declaration, the General Assembly reaffirmed that States have the duty to cooperate with one another, irrespective of the differences in their political, economic and social systems, in the various spheres of international relations, in order to maintain international peace and security and to promote international stability and progress, the general welfare of nations and international cooperation free from discrimination based on such differences.

To this end States are required to co-operate with other States in the maintenance of international peace and security. States must co-operate in the promotion of universal respect for, and observance of, human rights and fundamental freedoms for all, and in the elimination of all forms of racial discrimination and all forms of religious intolerance; States must conduct their international relations in the economic, social, cultural, technical and trade fields in accordance with the principles of sovereign equality and non-intervention; States members of the United Nations have the duty to take joint and separate action in cooperation with the United Nations in accordance with the relevant provisions of the Charter.

3 B. Simma (Ed.), *The Charter of the United Nations. A Commentary* (Oxford: Oxford University Press, 1985), pp. 55–56.

4 *Ibid.*, p. 794.

Furthermore, States must co-operate in the economic, social and cultural fields, as well as in the field of science and technology, and for the promotion of international cultural and educational progress. States must co-operate in the promotion of economic growth throughout the world, especially that of the developing countries.[5]

In the human rights literature, there is considerable discussion about the legal relationship between the UN Charter and the Universal Declaration of Human Rights, with some taking the position that the Universal Declaration is an authoritative elaboration on the human rights principles of the Charter.[6] In this book, we submit that Member States of the United Nations have three fundamental legal duties under the Charter:

(i) First to have in place, in their own countries, an adequate and effective national human rights protection system;
(ii) Second, a duty to cooperate with the United Nations in its actions for the promotion and protection of human rights world-wide; and
(iii) Third, a legal duty to comply with: treaties they have voluntarily ratified or adhered to, universally-binding human rights norms of customary international law, norms of *jus cogens;* and norms that may be derived from general principles derived from the principal legal systems of the world.

In a later chapter, we also submit that large parts of the Universal Declaration of Human Rights have now entered the body of universally-binding customary international law.

3 International Legality

In its draft articles on State responsibility, the International Law Commission included the following provision in Article 3:

> The characterization of an act of State as internationally wrongful is governed by international law. Such characterization is not affected by the characterization of the same act as lawful by internal law.

This article was first proposed by the Commission's then Special Rapporteur, Roberto Ago, and discussed in the Commission in 1973.[7] When the

5 GA Resolution 2625 (XXV), (24 October 1970).

6 This discussion is helpfully summarised in Theodor Meron, *Human Rights and Humanitarian Norms as Customary Law*. Oxford, Oxford University Press, 1989. See esp. Chapter II, "Human Rights Instruments and Customary Law".

7 The article was discussed at the 1209th and 1210th meetings of the Commission in 1973.

article was discussed in the Commission at its 1209th and 1210th meetings in 1973 the principle contained in it received support from every member of the Commission who took part in the discussion: Commisioners Ramangasoavina, Tsuruoka, Yasseen, Kearney, Sette Camara, Hambro, Ushakov, Elias, Vallat, Bartos, Ustor, Castaneda, Tammes, Bilge and Reuter.

In drafting the article, the Commission followed its own draft on the rights and duties of States, as well as Article 27 of the Vienna Convention on the Law of Treaties, which provided that "A party may not invoke the provisions of its internal law as justification for its failure to perform a treaty."

In the case of *R. v. Hape*,[8] the Supreme Court of Canada provided useful guidance on the place of customary international law in the domestic law of States, in this particular instance, Canada. The Supreme Court stated that international custom, as the law of nations, was also the law of Canada unless, "in a valid exercise of its sovereignty, Canada declared that its law was to the contrary."[9] In the assessment of Glen Linder:

> The majority … appears to endorse the view that if the rule of customary international law changes, so too will domestic law. Apparently endorsing the relevant passage from Lord Denning's landmark judgment in *Trendtex*[10] our highest court has now clarified that even where a common law precedent exists that is contrary to a newer customary international law rule, courts must follow the customary international law rule, and not the inconsistent common law precedent.[11]

In their decision, the majority of judges held that if the legislature wished to enact legislation inconsistent with international law, there must be "unequivocal legislative intent to default on an international obligation."

There is also respectable Commonwealth precedent for the proposition that where there is uncertainty, international law may be used in ascertaining the meaning of national legislation, for example in the interpretation of human rights and fundamental freedoms.[12]

---

8 (2007) SCC 26.

9 *Ibid.*, paras. 37–39.

10 *Trendtex Trading Corp v. Central Bank of Nigeria*, (1977) 1 Q.B., p. 529.

11 Glen Linder, Canadian Council of International Law, Case Comment, *R. v. Hape* – The International Law Aspects.

12 See *e.g.* The Bangalore Principles on the Domestic Application of International Human Rights Norms. On this, also see *e.g.* a speech by Justice Michael Kirby, "The First Ten Years of the Bangalore Principles on the Domestic Application of International Human Rights Norms" (available online).

4 The Supremacy of International Human Rights Law

The primacy of the supremacy of international law – and therefore the supremacy of international human rights law – over municipal law has been included in the following provisions either drafted or subsequently accepted by the International Law Commission: Articles 13 and 14 of the Draft Declaration on Rights and Duties of States; Articles 27, 46, 53, 64 of the Vienna Convention on the Law of Treaties (1969), and ILC draft Article 3 on State Responsibility.

The Preamble of the Draft Declaration on the Rights and Duties of States proclaimed that "the States of the world form a community governed by international law." According to Article 13 of the Draft Declaration, "Every State has the duty to carry out in good faith its obligations arising from treaties and other sources of international law, and it may not invoke provisions in its constitution or its laws as an excuse for failure to perform this duty." According to Article 14, "Every State has the duty to conduct its relations with other States in accordance with international law and with the principle that the sovereignty of each State is subject to the supremacy of international law." This principle was based on postulate 4 of the "International Law of the Future", published by the Carnegie Endowment for International Peace in 1944.

The International Law Commission approved these articles without any debate on their substance. The principles contained in them were taken as self-evident by the Commission. Commissioner Alfaro, in the draft he had prepared, which was used as the basis of discussion in the Commission, commented on these provisions as follows: Article 14 "deals with the authority of international law including everything agreed upon in the Charter of the United Nations and in the Statute of the World Court, which are international treaty law." Article 14 "proclaims that international law is obligatory for all States."[13] In the written comments of governments, the principle was accepted and, on the whole, taken as self-evident.[14]

Sir Gerald Fitzmaurice, in his course of lectures at the Hague Academy of International Law on "The General Principles of International Law Considered from the Standpoint of the Rule of Law", took as his starting point Article 14 of the International Law Commission's draft on Rights and Duties of States, which he commented upon as follows:

---

13 *Preparatory Study Concerning a Draft Declaration on the Rights and Duties of States*, A/CN.4/2, (15 December, 1948), p. 43.

14 *Ibid.* See the written comments of Mexico, p. 86, the United Kingdom, p. 86, Venezuela, p. 88.

> This provision enunciates the important principle of the subordination of the sovereignty of each State to the supremacy of international law – in short, of the sovereignty of the rule of law in the international field which might indeed be called the first and greatest principle of international law. From it all the rest follows: without it there may be customs, practices, habits, courtesies… but there is no law.[15]

Sir Gerald proceeded to demonstrate that this principle applied automatically, and that at the back of the principle, the ultimate source or basis of legal obligation in international law rested in the explanation of law as a social necessity.

Professor Hans Kelsen, while making some criticism of the actual formulation of this principle by the International Law Commission, accepted it as part of general international law. The duty laid down in Article 14, he felt, "is implied in the concept of international law. … The concept of international law implies the duty of every State to behave in all its relations in accordance with international law."[16]

He explained this more fully elsewhere:

> There is, above the commonwealth described as the State, a legal order which defines the respective scopes of power of individual States by forbidding the encroachment of one into the sphere of another… a legal order which regulates the relations of States by means of rules equally applicable to all. International law does this –but only when its supremacy over the legal systems of individual States is recognized, when… it is contemplated as a legal system standing above the States, i.e. when the legal systems of individual States are regarded as component parts of a universal legal order.[17]

Principle I of the Principles of International law Recognized in the Charter of the Nuremberg Tribunal and in the Judgment of the Tribunal, as consolidated by the International Law Commission, stated that any person who committed an act which constituted a crime under international law was responsible for it and liable to punishment. In the commentary to Principle 1, the International Law Commission clarified that the general rule

---

15 Sir Gerald Fitzmaurice, Q.C., "The General Principles of International Law Considered from the Standpoint of the Rule of Law", 92 *RCADI* (1957, II), p. 6.

16 H. Kelsen, "The Draft Declaration of Rights and Duties of States", 44 *American Journal of International Law* (1950), pp. 259–276.

17 *Der Begriff der Souveranitat und die Theorie des Volkerrechts* (1920), cited in H. Lauterpacht, *Private Law Sources and Analogies of International Law* (1933), p. 5.

underlying it was that international law may impose duties on individuals directly without any interposition of internal law. Principle II stated that the fact that internal law does not impose a penalty for an act which constitutes a crime under international law does not relieve the persons who committed the act from responsibility under international law. In its commentary on this principle the International Law Commission observed that "The principle that a person who has committed an international crime is responsible therefor, and liable to punishment under international law, independently of the provisions of internal law, implies what is commonly called the 'supremacy of international law over national law."[18]

The Commission's draft articles on *jus cogens*, which became Articles 53 and 64 of the Vienna Convention on the Law of Treaties, were also clearly based on the assumption that international law overrides municipal law in matters of international public policy.

5 The Universality of International Humanitarian Law

In 2005, the International Committee of the Red Cross (ICRC), fulfilling a mandate entrusted to it by the International Red Cross and Red Crescent Conference, published a landmark publication, *Customary International Humanitarian Law*, a codification of the main rules of international humanitarian law. It contained 161 succinct rules of the binding norms applicable in all armed conflicts, international and non-international. In a Foreword to the publication, the then President of the ICRC, Dr Jakob Kellenberger, commented that it had served to emphasize the universality of humanitarian law. All traditions and civilizations had contributed in the development of this law, which is today part of the common heritage of mankind.[19]

The 161 rules summarized in the volume are cast in the form of numerous kinds of prohibited conduct in warfare, the duty to take particular care, to take all possible measures, to undertake special efforts to respect and protect those at risk, and in some instances, to take measures to prevent particular harm. The rules deal with the principle of distinction, specifically protected persons and objects, specific methods of warfare, weapons, treatment of civilians, and implementation. The chapter on implementation deals with compliance with international humanitarian law, enforcement of international humanitarian law, responsibility and reparation, individual responsibility, and war crimes.

---

18 ILC Report 1950, para. 102 of Commentary to Principle II, *YBILC* 1950, Vol. II, p. 375.

19 ICRC, *Customary Humanitarian Law* (2005), p. xi.

The year of publication of the volume, 2005, was the year in which the United Nations General Assembly, endorsed the Responsibility to Protect concept, with its three dimensions: the responsibility to prevent, the responsibility to react, and the responsibility to rebuild. The Independent Commission on Intervention and State Sovereignty, which advocated the concept of the responsibility to protect, considered the responsibility to prevent to be the nub of the responsibility to protect. A question that immediately arises for reflection is how the responsibility to protect, and in particular the responsibility to prevent, is pertinent to international humanitarian law.

Rule 142 of the ICRC rules provides that States parties to a conflict must provide instruction in international humanitarian law to their armed forces and this has a preventive rationale. So does Rule 149: A state is responsible for violations of international humanitarian law attributable to it. Likewise, Rule 151: Individuals are criminally responsible for war crimes they commit, and Rule 154: Every combatant has a duty to disobey a manifestly unlawful order. Rule 156 clarifies that serious violations of international humanitarian law constitute war crimes. Likewise, Rule 157: States have the right to vest universal jurisdiction in their national courts over war crimes. Rule 161 clarifies that statutes of limitation may not apply to war crimes, while Rule 161 adds that States must make every effort to cooperate, to the extent possible, with each other in order to facilitate the investigation of war crimes and the prosecution of the suspects.

From the point of view of the substantive content of international humanitarian law, it would seem that following General Assembly and Security Council endorsement of the responsibility to protect concept, the following preventive rules of international humanitarian law could be supported:

- States have the duty to do everything possible to prevent wars.
- States have the duty to act for the prevention of violations of international humanitarian law.
- The Security Council has the duty to act for the prevention of violations of international humanitarian law.
- Competent International Organizations have the duty to do everything possible to help prevent armed conflicts.
- Competent International Organizations have the duty to act for the prevention of violations of international humanitarian law.
- The International Committee of the Red Cross has a duty to act for the prevention of violations of international humanitarian law.

6 Mandatory Decisions of the United Nations Security Council

Under Article 24, Paragraph 1 of the United Nations Charter, Members of the United Nations, in order to ensure prompt and effective action by the United Nations, confer on the Security Council primary responsibility for the maintenance of international peace and security and agree that in carrying out its duties under this responsibility the Security Council acts on their behalf.

The International Court of Justice, in the Expenses Case and the 'Wall Case', has taken the view that since, under Article 24 of the United Nations Charter, the Security Council has the primary responsibility for the maintenance of international peace and security, it can, in that regard impose on States "an explicit obligation of compliance if for example it issues an order or command... under Chapter VII" of the Charter. The Council can, to that end, "require enforcement by coercive action".[20] The late Professor Ian Brownlie had pointed out that "When competent organs of the United Nations make a binding determination that a situation is illegal, the states which are the addressees of the resolution or resolutions concerned are under an obligation to bring that situation to an end."[21]

According to Article 43 of the Charter, all Members of the United Nations, in order to contribute to the maintenance of international peace and security, undertake to make available to the Security Council, on its call and in accordance with a special agreement or agreements, armed forces, assistance and facilities, including rights of passage necessary for the purpose of maintaining international peace and security.

The mandatory decisions of the Security Council on anti-terrorism measures, adopted under Chapter VII of the Charter, provide solid examples of actions required by Member States within their national legal orders.

7 Conclusion

This chapter has shown that, under the UN Charter, every government has legal duties to uphold human rights within its own jurisdiction, to have in place an adequate and effective national human rights protection system, and to cooperate with the United Nations in upholding human rights

20 *Certain Expenses of the United Nations* (Article 17, paragraph 2 of the Charter), Advisory Opinion of 20 July 1962, ICJ Reports 1962, p. 163. *Legal Consequences of the Construction of a Wall in the Occupied Palestinian Territory*, Advisory Opinion, ICJ Reports 2004, para. 26.

21 Brownlie, *op. cit.*, Second Edition, p. 504.

everywhere in the world. This was explicitly affirmed in the Declaration on Principles of International Law Concerning Friendly Relations and Co-operation Among States. We have also seen that the obligations of a State under international law take precedence over any contrary national law or obligation. And we have seen that the substantive content of international law is to be determined in accordance with the tests of international law itself, rather than any national test.

What all of this means is that every Government in the world is legally obliged to act for the upholding of human rights within its own jurisdiction as well in the world at large. In order words, the responsibility to uphold universal human rights norms is itself universal, that is to say, binding on all Governments.

4 The Legal Obligations Undertaken by States Parties under Treaties: General Comment No. 31 of the Human Rights Committee

1 Introduction

In this chapter we present General Comment No. 31 of the UN Human Rights Committee on the legal obligations of a State that has ratified a human rights treaty such as the International Covenant on Civil and Political Rights (1966).

2 General Comment No. 31 of the UN Human Rights Committee

General Comment No. 31 adopted by the Human Rights Committee on 26 May 2004 is a superb statement of the nature of human rights treaty obligations. A State Party, the Committee declared, must respect and ensure the rights in the Covenant to anyone within its power or effective control. The obligations in the Covenant in general, and under Article 2 in particular, are binding on every State Party as a whole. All branches of government (executive, legislative and judicial), and other public or governmental authorities, at whatever level – national, regional or local – are in a position to engage the responsibility of the State Party.

States Parties must adopt legislative, judicial, administrative, educative and other appropriate measures in order to fulfil their legal obligations. It is important to raise levels of awareness about the Covenant not only among public officials and state agents but also among the population at large.

The positive obligations on States Parties to ensure Covenant rights will only be discharged if individuals are protected by the state not just against violations of Covenant rights by its agents, but also against acts committed by private persons or entities that would impair the enjoyment of Covenant rights in so far as they are amenable to application between private persons or entities. There may be circumstances in which a failure to ensure Covenant rights as required by Article 2 would give rise to violations by States Parties of those rights as a result of States Parties' permitting or failing to take appropriate measures or to exercise due diligence to prevent, punish, investigate or redress the harm caused by such acts by private persons or entities. States Parties have a duty to address the activities of private persons or entities such as the duty to ensure that private persons or entities do not inflict torture.

States Parties are required to respect and to ensure the Covenant rights to all persons who may be within their territory and to all persons subject to their jurisdiction. This means that a State Party must respect and ensure the rights laid down in the Covenant to anyone within the power or effective control of that State Party, even if not situated within the territory of the State Party. The enjoyment of Covenant rights is not limited to citizens of States Parties, but must also be available to all individuals, regardless of nationality or statelessness, such as asylum seekers, refugees, migrant workers and other persons who may find themselves in the territory or subject to the jurisdiction of the State Party. This principle also applies to those within the power or effective control of the forces of a State Party acting outside its territory, regardless of the circumstances in which such power or effective control was obtained, such as forces constituting a national contingent of a State Party assigned to an international peacekeeping or peace-enforcement operation.

The Covenant applies also in situations of armed conflict to which the rules of international humanitarian law are applicable. While, in respect of certain Covenant rights, more specific rules of international humanitarian law may be specially relevant for the purposes of the interpretation of Covenant rights, both spheres of law are complementary, not mutually exclusive.

Article 2, paragraph 2 of the Covenant requires that States Parties take the necessary steps to give effect to the Covenant rights in the domestic order. It follows that, unless the Covenant's rights are already protected by their domestic law or practices, States Parties are required on ratification to make such changes to domestic laws and practices as are necessary to ensure their conformity with the Covenant. Where there are inconsistencies between domestic law and the Covenant, Article 2 requires that the domestic law or practice be changed to meet the standards required by the Covenant's substantive guarantees.

Article 2 allows a State Party to pursue this in accordance with its own domestic constitutional structure and accordingly does not require that the Covenant be directly applicable in the courts by incorporation of the Covenant into national laws. The Committee takes the view, however, that Covenant guarantees may receive enhanced protection in those states where the Covenant is automatically or through specific incorporation part of the domestic legal order. The Committee invited those States Parties in which the Covenant did not form part of the domestic legal order to consider incorporation of the Covenant to render it part of domestic law to facilitate full realization of Covenant rights as required by Article 2.

The requirement under Article 2, paragraph 2, to take steps to give effect to the Covenant rights is unqualified and of immediate effect. A failure to comply with this obligation cannot be justified by reference to political, social, cultural or economic considerations within the State.

Article 2, paragraph 3, requires that, in addition to effective protection of Covenant rights, States Parties must ensure that individuals also have accessible and effective remedies to vindicate those rights. Such remedies should be appropriately adapted so as to take account of the special vulnerability of certain categories of person, including in particular children. The Committee attaches importance to States Parties establishing appropriate judicial and administrative mechanisms for addressing claims of rights violations under domestic law.

Article 2, paragraph 3 of the Covenant requires that States Parties make reparation to individuals whose Covenant rights have been violated. Without reparation to individuals whose Covenant rights have been violated, the obligation to provide an effective remedy, which is central to the efficacy of Article 2, paragraph 3, is not discharged. In addition to the explicit reparation required by Article 9, paragraph 5, and Article 14, paragraph 6, the Committee considers that the Covenant generally, entails appropriate compensation. The Committee noted that, where appropriate, reparation can involve restitution, rehabilitation and measures of satisfaction, such as public apologies, public memorials, guarantees of non-repetition and changes in relevant laws and practices, as well as bringing to justice the perpetrators of human rights violations.

In general, the purposes of the Covenant would be defeated without an obligation integral to Article 2 to take measures to prevent the recurrence of a violation of the Covenant. Accordingly, it has been a frequent practice of the Committee, in its consideration of individual petitions under the Optional Protocol, to include in its Views the need for measures, beyond a victim-specific remedy, to be taken to avoid recurrence of the type of violation in question. Such measures may require changes in the State Party's laws or practices.

Where investigations reveal violations of certain Covenant rights, States Parties must ensure that those responsible are brought to justice. As with failure to investigate, failure to bring to justice perpetrators of such violations could in and of itself give rise to a separate breach of the Covenant. These obligations arise notably in respect of those violations recognized as criminal under either domestic or international law, such as torture and similar cruel, inhuman and degrading treatment (Article 7), summary and arbitrary killing (Article 6) and enforced disappearance (Articles 7 and 9 and frequently 6). Indeed, the problem of impunity for these violations, a matter of sustained concern by the Committee, might well be an important contributing element in the recurrence of the violations. When committed as part of a widespread or systematic attack on a civilian population, these violations of the Covenant are crimes against humanity (Rome Statute of the International Criminal Court (ICC), Article 7).

Accordingly, where public officials or state agents have committed violations of the Covenant rights, the States Parties concerned may not relieve perpetrators from personal responsibility. Furthermore, no official status justifies persons who may be accused of responsibility for such violations being held immune from legal responsibility. Other impediments to the establishment of legal responsibility should also be removed, such as the defence of obedience to superior orders or unreasonably short periods of statutory limitation in cases where such limitations are applicable. States Parties should also assist each other to bring to justice persons suspected of having committed acts in violation of the Covenant that are punishable under domestic or international law.

The Committee further took the view that the right to an effective remedy may in certain circumstances require States Parties to provide for and implement provisional or interim measures to avoid continuing violations and to endeavour to repair at the earliest possible opportunity any harm that may have been caused by such violations.

3 Conclusion

General Comment No. 31 is a solid reflection of the legal obligations of States under the Covenant and under international human rights treaties generally. Superimposed on all of this is the United Nations Charter, which has concrete legal obligations on every Member State to uphold universal human rights.

In a modern justice system, it must be right as a matter of principle that judges and lawyers have due regard to the legal obligations of governments under the international human rights treaties they have voluntarily agreed to be bound by. General Comment No. 31 of the UN Human Rights Committee provides helpful guidance for judges and lawyers to contribute to the effective implementation of the international treaty obligations of governments.

5 The UN Basic Principles and Guidelines on the Right to a Remedy and Reparation for Victims of Gross Violations of International Human Rights Law and Serious Violations of International Humanitarian Law

1 Introduction

In this chapter we look at the universal duty to provide redress as it has been codified in a set of UN principles endorsed by the UN General Assembly and as it has been expounded upon by human rights treaty bodies.

2 The UN Basic Principles and Guidelines

The Basic Principles and Guidelines on the issue of remedies and compensation, which the UN General Assembly adopted in 2006, provide an authoritative statement of the duty of Governments to provide remedies for human rights violations. The adoption of the Basic Principles and Guidelines followed years of study by independent experts and taking account of governmental comments.[1] The Basic Principles and Guidelines contain thirteen chapters with core provisions of international human rights law. Because of the clarity and firmness of the statements in the document, we summarize key provisions below. The document is a magisterial summary of the contemporary international law of human rights generally, and of the ideas of justice, redress and reparation in particular.

2.1 *Obligation to Respect, Ensure Respect for and Implement International Human Rights Law and International Humanitarian Law*

The Basic Principles and Guidelines recall that the obligation to respect, ensure respect for, and implement international human rights law and international humanitarian law as provided for under the respective bodies of law emanate from: treaties to which a State is a party; customary international law; the domestic law of each State. The document urges that if they have not already done so, States must, as required under international

1 General Assembly Resolution 60/147.

law, ensure that their domestic law is consistent with their international legal obligations by:

(a) Incorporating norms of international human rights law and international humanitarian law into their domestic law, or otherwise implementing them in their domestic legal system;
(b) Adopting appropriate and effective legislative and administrative procedures and other appropriate measures that provide fair, effective and prompt access to justice;
(c) Making available adequate, effective, prompt, and appropriate remedies, including reparation; and
(d) Ensuring that their domestic law provides at least the same level of protection for victims as required by their international obligations.

2.2 *Scope of the Obligation*

The Basic Principles and Guidelines specify that the obligation to respect, ensure respect for and implement international human rights law and international humanitarian law as provided for under the respective bodies of law, includes, inter alia, the duty to:

(a) Take appropriate legislative and administrative and other appropriate measures to prevent violations;
(b) Investigate violations effectively, promptly, thoroughly and impartially and, where appropriate, take action against those allegedly responsible in accordance with domestic and international law;
(c) Provide those who claim to be victims of a human rights or humanitarian law violation with equal and effective access to justice, as described below, irrespective of who may ultimately be the bearer of responsibility for the violation; and
(d) Provide effective remedies to victims, including reparation, as described below.

2.3 *Gross Violations of International Human Rights Law and Serious Violations of International Humanitarian Law that Constitute Crimes under International Law*

The Basic Principles and Guidelines underline that in cases of gross violations of international human rights law and serious violations of international humanitarian law constituting crimes under international law, States have the duty to investigate and, if there is sufficient evidence, the duty to submit to prosecution the person allegedly responsible for the violations and, if found guilty, the duty to punish her or him. Moreover, in these cases, States should, in accordance with international law, cooperate with one another and assist international judicial organs competent in the investigation and prosecution of these violations.

To this end, where so provided in an applicable treaty or under other international law obligations, States must incorporate or otherwise implement within their domestic law appropriate provisions for universal jurisdiction. Moreover, where it is so provided for in an applicable treaty or other international legal obligations, States must facilitate extradition or surrender offenders to other States and to appropriate international judicial bodies and provide judicial assistance and other forms of cooperation in the pursuit of international justice, including assistance to, and protection of, victims and witnesses, consistent with international human rights legal standards and subject to international legal requirements such as those relating to the prohibition of torture and other forms of cruel, inhuman or degrading treatment or punishment.

2.4 *Statutes of Limitations*

The Basic Principles and Guidelines specify that where so provided for in an applicable treaty or contained in other international legal obligations, statutes of limitations shall not apply to gross violations of international human rights law and serious violations of international humanitarian law which constitute crimes under international law. Domestic statutes of limitations for other types of violations that do not constitute crimes under international law, including those time limitations applicable to civil claims and other procedures, should not be unduly restrictive.

2.5 *Victims of Gross Violations of International Human Rights Law and Serious Violations of International Humanitarian Law*

The Basic Principles and Guidelines defines victims as persons who individually or collectively suffered harm, including physical or mental injury, emotional suffering, economic loss or substantial impairment of their fundamental rights, through acts or omissions that constitute gross violations of international human rights law, or serious violations of international humanitarian law. Where appropriate, and in accordance with domestic law, the term "victim" also includes the immediate family or dependants of the direct victim and persons who have suffered harm in intervening to assist victims in distress or to prevent victimization. A person shall be considered a victim regardless of whether the perpetrator of the violation is identified, apprehended, prosecuted, or convicted and regardless of the familial relationship between the perpetrator and the victim.

2.6 *Treatment of Victims*

The Basic Principles and Guidelines specifies that victims should be treated with humanity and respect for their dignity and human rights, and appropriate measures should be taken to ensure their safety, physical and psychological wellbeing and privacy, as well as those of their families. The State should ensure that its domestic laws, to the extent possible, provide that a victim who has suffered violence or trauma should benefit from special consideration and care to avoid his or her retraumatization in the course of legal and administrative procedures designed to provide justice and reparation.

2.7 *Victims' Right to Remedies*

The Basic Principles and Guidelines include as remedies for gross violations of international human rights law and serious violations of international humanitarian law the victim's right to the following as provided for under international law: equal and effective access to justice; adequate, effective and prompt reparation for harm suffered; and access to relevant information concerning violations and reparation mechanisms.

2.8 *Access to Justice*

The Basic Principles and Guidelines register that a victim of a gross violation of international human rights law or of a serious violation of international humanitarian law must have equal access to an effective judicial remedy as provided for under international law. Other remedies available to the victim include access to administrative and other bodies, as well as mechanisms, modalities and proceedings conducted in accordance with domestic law. Obligations arising under international law to secure the right to access justice and fair and impartial proceedings shall be reflected in domestic laws. To that end, States should:

(a) Disseminate, through public and private mechanisms, information about all available remedies for gross violations of international human rights law and serious violations of international humanitarian law;
(b) Take measures to minimize the inconvenience to victims and their representatives, protect against unlawful interference with their privacy as appropriate and ensure their safety from intimidation and retaliation, as well as that of their families and witnesses, before, during and after judicial, administrative, or other proceedings that affect the interests of victims;
(c) Provide proper assistance to victims seeking access to justice;
(d) Make available all appropriate legal, diplomatic and consular means to ensure that victims can exercise their rights to remedy for gross

violations of international human rights law or serious violations of international humanitarian law.

In addition to individual access to justice, States must endeavour to develop procedures to allow groups of victims to present claims for reparation and to receive reparation, as appropriate. An adequate, effective and prompt remedy for gross violations of international human rights law or serious violations of international humanitarian law must include all available and appropriate international processes in which a person may have legal standing and should be without prejudice to any other domestic remedies.

2.9 *Reparation for Harm Suffered*

The Basic Principles and Guidelines stipulate that adequate, effective and prompt reparation is intended to promote justice by redressing gross violations of international human rights law or serious violations of international humanitarian law. Reparation should be proportional to the gravity of the violations and the harm suffered. In accordance with its domestic laws and international legal obligations, a State shall provide reparation to victims for acts or omissions which can be attributed to the State and constitute gross violations of international human rights law or serious violations of international humanitarian law. In cases where a person, a legal person, or other entity is found liable for reparation to a victim, such party should provide reparation to the victim or compensate the State if the State has already provided reparation to the victim.

States should endeavour to establish national programmes for reparation and other assistance to victims in the event that the party liable for the harm suffered is unable or unwilling to meet their obligations. States shall, with respect to claims by victims, enforce domestic judgments for reparation against individuals or entities liable for the harm suffered and endeavour to enforce valid foreign legal judgments for reparation in accordance with domestic law and international legal obligations. To that end, States should provide under their domestic laws effective mechanisms for the enforcement of reparation judgments.

In accordance with domestic law and international law, and taking account of individual circumstances, victims of gross violations of international human rights law and serious violations of international humanitarian law must, as appropriate and proportional to the gravity of the violation and the circumstances of each case, be provided with full and effective reparation, as laid out in principles 19 to 23, which include the following forms: restitution, compensation, rehabilitation, satisfaction and guarantees of nonrepetition.

Restitution should, whenever possible, restore the victim to the original situation before the gross violations of international human rights law or serious violations of international humanitarian law occurred. Restitution includes, as appropriate: restoration of liberty, enjoyment of human rights, identity, family life and citizenship, return to one's place of residence, restoration of employment and return of property.

Compensation should be provided for any economically assessable damage, as appropriate and proportional to the gravity of the violation and the circumstances of each case, resulting from gross violations of international human rights law and serious violations of international humanitarian law, such as:

(a) Physical or mental harm;
(b) Lost opportunities, including employment, education and social benefits;
(c) Material damages and loss of earnings, including loss of earning potential;
(d) Moral damage;
(e) Costs required for legal or expert assistance, medicine and medical services, and psychological and social services.

Rehabilitation should include medical and psychological care as well as legal and social services. Satisfaction should include, where applicable, any or all of the following:

(a) Effective measures aimed at the cessation of continuing violations;
(b) Verification of the facts and full and public disclosure of the truth to the extent that such disclosure does not cause further harm or threaten the safety and interests of the victim, the victim's relatives, witnesses, or persons who have intervened to assist the victim or prevent the occurrence of further violations;
(c) The search for the whereabouts of the disappeared, for the identities of the children abducted, and for the bodies of those killed, and assistance in the recovery, identification and reburial of the bodies in accordance with the expressed or presumed wish of the victims, or the cultural practices of the families and communities;
(d) An official declaration or a judicial decision restoring the dignity, the reputation and the rights of the victim and of persons closely connected with the victim;
(e) Public apology, including acknowledgement of the facts and acceptance of responsibility;
(f) Judicial and administrative sanctions against persons liable for the violations;
(g) Commemorations and tributes to the victims;

(h) Inclusion of an accurate account of the violations that occurred in international human rights law and international humanitarian law training and in educational material at all levels.

Guarantees of nonrepetition should include, where applicable, any or all of the following measures, which will also contribute to prevention:

(a) Ensuring effective civilian control of military and security forces;
(b) Ensuring that all civilian and military proceedings abide by international standards of due process, fairness and impartiality;
(c) Strengthening the independence of the judiciary;
(d) Protecting persons in the legal, medical and healthcare professions, the media and other related professions, and human rights defenders;
(e) Providing, on a priority and continued basis, human rights and international humanitarian law education to all sectors of society and training for law enforcement officials as well as military and security forces;
(f) Promoting the observance of codes of conduct and ethical norms, in particular international standards, by public servants, including law enforcement, correctional, media, medical, psychological, social service and military personnel, as well as by economic enterprises;
(g) Promoting mechanisms for preventing and monitoring social conflicts and their resolution;
(h) Reviewing and reforming laws contributing to or allowing gross violations of international human rights law and serious violations of international humanitarian law.

2.10 *Access to Relevant Information Concerning Violations and Reparation Mechanisms*

The Basic Principles and Guidelines call upon States to develop means of informing the general public and, in particular, victims of gross violations of international human rights law and serious violations of international humanitarian law of the rights and remedies addressed by these Principles and Guidelines and of all available legal, medical, psychological, social, administrative and all other services to which victims may have a right of access. Moreover, victims and their representatives should be entitled to seek and obtain information on the causes leading to their victimization and on the causes and conditions pertaining to the gross violations of international human rights law and serious violations of international humanitarian law and to learn the truth in regard to these violations.

2.11 *Non Discrimination*

The Basic Principles and Guidelines underline that the application and interpretation of its provisions must be consistent with international human rights law and international humanitarian law and be without any discrimination of any kind or ground, without exception.

3 The Jurisprudence and Practice of Treaty Bodies

We set out next some of the relevant pronouncements of human rights treaty bodies on the duty to provide remedies.

3.1 *Inter-American Court of Human Rights*

In its Advisory Opinion on Judicial Guarantees in States of Emergency[2] the Inter-American Court of Human Rights underlined the importance of the principle of effective judicial remedies to victims of human rights violations and declared as follows:

> According to this principle, the absence of an effective remedy to violations of the rights recognized by the Convention is itself a violation of the Convention by the State Party in which the remedy is lacking. In that sense, it should be emphasized that, for such a remedy to exist, it is not sufficient that it be provided for by the Constitution or by law or that it be formally recognized, but rather it must be truly effective in establishing whether there has been a violation of human rights and in providing redress. A remedy which proves illusory because of the general conditions prevailing in the country, or even in the particular circumstances of a given case, cannot be considered effective. That could be the case, for example, when practice has shown its ineffectiveness, when the Judicial Power lacks the necessary independence to render impartial decisions or the means to carry out its judgments; or in any other situation that constitutes a denial of justice, as when there is an unjustified delay in the decision or when, for any reason, the alleged victim is denied access to a judicial remedy.[3]

3.2 *Human Rights Committee*

The Human Rights Committee, in its General Comment No. 31 provided the following guidance on the issue of remedies:

---

2 Advisory Opinion OC-9/87 of October 6, 1987, Series A No. 9.

3 Para. 24.

> Article 2, paragraph 3, requires that in addition to effective protection of Covenant rights States parties must ensure that individuals also have accessible and effective remedies to vindicate those rights. Such remedies should be appropriately adapted so as to take account of the special vulnerability of certain categories of person, including in particular children. The Committee attaches importance to States parties' establishing appropriate judicial and administrative mechanisms for addressing claims of rights violations under domestic law. The Committee notes that the enjoyment of the rights recognized under the Covenant can be effectively assured by the judiciary in many different ways, including direct applicability of the Covenant, application of comparable constitutional or other provisions of law, or the interpretive effect of the Covenant in the application of national law. Administrative mechanisms are particularly required to give effect to the general obligation to investigate allegations of violations promptly, thoroughly and effectively through independent and impartial bodies. National human rights institutions, endowed with appropriate powers, can contribute to this end. A failure by a State party to investigate allegations of violations could in and of itself give rise to a separate breach of the Covenant. Cessation of an ongoing violation is an essential element of the right to an effective remedy.[4]

3.3 *Committee on Economic, Social and Cultural Rights*

The Committee on Economic, Social and Cultural Rights has taken the view that:

> The right to an effective remedy need not be interpreted as always requiring a judicial remedy. Administrative remedies will, in many cases, be adequate and those living within the jurisdiction of a State party have a legitimate expectation, based on the principle of good faith, that all administrative authorities will take account of the requirements of the Covenant in their decision-making. Any such administrative remedies should be accessible, affordable, timely and effective. An ultimate right of judicial appeal from administrative procedures of this type would also often be appropriate. By the same token, there are some obligations, such as (but by no means limited to) those concerning non-discrimination in relation to which the provision of some form of judicial remedy would seem indispensable in

4 General Comment No. 31, HRI/GEN/Rev.9 p. 246.

order to satisfy the requirements of the Covenant. In other words, whenever a Covenant right cannot be made fully effective without some role for the judiciary, judicial remedies are necessary.[5]

3.4 *Committee on the Elimination of Discrimination against Women (CEDAW)*

CEDAW has provided the following guidance. "Measures that are necessary to overcome family violence should include:

- Criminal penalties where necessary and civil remedies in case of domestic violence;
- Legislation to remove the defence of honour in regard to the assault or murder of a female family member;
- Services to ensure the safety and security of victims of family violence, including refuges, counselling and rehabilitation programmes;
- Rehabilitation programmes for perpetrators of domestic violence;
- Support services for families where incest or sexual abuse has occurred."[6]

3.5 *Committee on the Elimination of Racial Discrimination (CERD)*

The Committee on the Elimination of Racial Discrimination (CERD) has adopted the following position:

> The Committee notifies States parties that, in its opinion, the right to seek just and adequate reparation or satisfaction for any damage suffered as a result of such discrimination, which is embodies in article 6 of the Convention, is not necessarily secured solely by the punishment of the perpetrator of the discrimination; at the same time, the courts and other competent authorities should consider awarding financial compensation for damage, material or moral, suffered by a victim, whenever appropriate.[7]

4. **Conclusion**

The UN Basic Principles and Guidelines, and the pronouncements of human rights treaty bodies all underscore the universal duty of Governments to provide appropriate remedies for violations of human rights. We have set out the provisions of the Basic Principles and Guidelines as a frame of

5 General Comment No. 9, HRI/GEN/Rev.9, p. 49.
6 General Recommendation No. 19, HRI/GEN/Rev.9, p. 336.
7 General Recommendation XXVI, HRI/GEN/Rev.9, p. 288.

reference for judges and lawyers. We have adduced the recommendations of human rights treaty bodies to provide indications of what they consider would be useful for strengthening remedies and reparations for violations of human rights.

6 The UN Basic Principles on the Independence of the Judiciary

1 Introduction

In this chapter we present the UN Basic Principles on the Independence of the Judiciary. Before doing so, we refer to some principles pioneered by the International Commission of Jurists.

2 Principles Developed by the International Commission of Jurists

Ever since its inception, the International Commission of Jurists has elaborated a series of principles that provided guidance on the practical meaning of the rule of law. These included the following:

2.1 *Essential Requirements of a Society under the Rule of Law*

- The legislative power must be effectively exercised by an appropriate organ, freely elected by the citizens. The laws and other legal measures taken by the legislative cannot be abolished or restricted by a governmental measure.
- The Rule of Law can only reach its highest expression and fullest realization under representative government. By representative government is meant a government deriving its power and authority from the people, which power and authority are exercised through representatives freely chosen and responsible to them. Free periodic elections are therefore important to representative government.

2.2 *The Legislature and the Rule of Law*

- The function of the legislature in a free society under the Rule of Law is to create and maintain the conditions which will uphold the dignity of the human being as an individual. This dignity requires not only the recognition of his or her civil and political rights but also the establishment of the social, economic, educational and cultural conditions which are essential to the full development of his or her personality. Every legislature in a free society under the Rule of Law should endeavour to give full effect to the principles enunciated in the Universal Declaration of Human Rights.

2.2 *The Executive and the Rule of Law*

- In general, the acts of the executive which directly and injuriously affect the person or property or rights of the individual should be subject to review by the courts.

- It will further the Rule of Law if the executive is required to formulate its reasons when reaching its decisions of a judicial or administrative character and affecting the rights of individuals and at the request of a party concerned to communicate them to him.

2.4 *The Criminal Process and the Rule of Law*

- It is always important that the definition and interpretation of the law should be as certain as possible, and this is of particular importance in the case of the criminal law, where the citizen's life or liberty may be at stake.

2.5 *The Judiciary and the Rule of Law*

- An independent judiciary is an indispensable requisite of a free society under the Rule of Law.

2.6 *The Legal Profession and the Rule of Law*

- It is essential to the maintenance of the Rule of Law that there should be an organized legal profession free to manage its own affairs. But it is recognized that there may be general supervision by the courts and that there may be regulations governing the admission to, and pursuit of, the legal profession.
- Lawyers should refuse to collaborate with any authority in any action which violates the Rule of Law. Lawyers should endeavour to promote knowledge of, and to inspire respect for, the Rule of Law, and an appreciation by all people of their rights under the law.

2.7 *Economic and Social Development*

- It is essential to economic and social development to overcome inequality arising from birth or wealth and discrimination.

2.8 *ICJ Declaration at Its 2019 Triennial Congress*

The Declaration of the International Commission of Jurists at its 2019 triennial congress is appended at the end of this book.

3 The UN Basic Principles on the Independence of the Judiciary (1985)[1]

We reproduce the UN Basic Principles on the Independence of the Judiciary (1985) below:

> Whereas in the Charter of the United Nations the peoples of the world affirm, inter alia , their determination to establish conditions under which justice can be maintained to achieve international co-operation in promoting and encouraging respect for human rights and fundamental freedoms without any discrimination,
>
> Whereas the Universal Declaration of Human Rights enshrines in particular the principles of equality before the law, of the presumption of innocence and of the right to a fair and public hearing by a competent, independent and impartial tribunal established by law,
>
> Whereas the International Covenants on Economic, Social and Cultural Rights and on Civil and Political Rights both guarantee the exercise of those rights, and in addition, the Covenant on Civil and Political Rights further guarantees the right to be tried without undue delay,
>
> Whereas frequently there still exists a gap between the vision underlying those principles and the actual situation,
>
> Whereas the organization and administration of justice in every country should be inspired by those principles, and efforts should be undertaken to translate them fully into reality,
>
> Whereas rules concerning the exercise of judicial office should aim at enabling judges to act in accordance with those principles,
>
> Whereas judges are charged with the ultimate decision over life, freedoms, rights, duties and property of citizens,
>
> Whereas the Sixth United Nations Congress on the Prevention of Crime and the Treatment of Offenders, by its resolution 16, called upon the Committee on Crime Prevention and Control to include among its priorities the elaboration of guidelines relating to the independence of judges and the selection, professional training and status of judges and prosecutors,
>
> Whereas it is, therefore, appropriate that consideration be first given to the role of judges in relation to the system of justice and to the

---

1 Adopted by the Seventh United Nations Congress on the Prevention of Crime and the Treatment of Offenders held at Milan from 26 August to 6 September 1985 and endorsed by General Assembly Resolutions 40/32 of 29 November 1985 and 40/146 of 13 December 1985.

importance of their selection, training and conduct,

The following basic principles, formulated to assist Member States in their task of securing and promoting the independence of the judiciary should be taken into account and respected by Governments within the framework of their national legislation and practice and be brought to the attention of judges, lawyers, members of the executive and the legislature and the public in general. The principles have been formulated principally with professional judges in mind, but they apply equally, as appropriate, to lay judges, where they exist.

Independence of the Judiciary

1. The independence of the judiciary shall be guaranteed by the State and enshrined in the Constitution or the law of the country. It is the duty of all governmental and other institutions to respect and observe the independence of the judiciary.
2. The judiciary shall decide matters before them impartially, on the basis of facts and in accordance with the law, without any restrictions, improper influences, inducements, pressures, threats or interferences, direct or indirect, from any quarter or for any reason.
3. The judiciary shall have jurisdiction over all issues of a judicial nature and shall have exclusive authority to decide whether an issue submitted for its decision is within its competence as defined by law.
4. There shall not be any inappropriate or unwarranted interference with the judicial process, nor shall judicial decisions by the courts be subject to revision. This principle is without prejudice to judicial review or to mitigation or commutation by competent authorities of sentences imposed by the judiciary, in accordance with the law.
5. Everyone shall have the right to be tried by ordinary courts or tribunals using established legal procedures. Tribunals that do not use the duly established procedures of the legal process shall not be created to displace the jurisdiction belonging to the ordinary courts or judicial tribunals.
6. The principle of the independence of the judiciary entitles and requires the judiciary to ensure that judicial proceedings are conducted fairly and that the rights of the parties are respected.
7. It is the duty of each Member State to provide adequate resources to enable the judiciary to properly perform its functions.

Freedom of Expression and Association

8. In accordance with the Universal Declaration of Human Rights, members of the judiciary are, like other citizens, entitled to freedom of expression, belief, association and assembly; provided, however, that in exercising such rights, judges shall always conduct themselves in such a manner as to preserve the dignity of their office and the impartiality and independence of the judiciary.
9. Judges shall be free to form and join associations of judges or other organizations to represent their interests, to promote their professional training and to protect their judicial independence.

Qualifications, Selection and Training

10. Persons selected for judicial office shall be individuals of integrity and ability with appropriate training or qualifications in law. Any method of judicial selection shall safeguard against judicial appointments for improper motives. In the selection of judges, there shall be no discrimination against a person on the grounds of race, colour, sex, religion, political or other opinion, national or social origin, property, birth or status, except that a requirement, that a candidate for judicial office must be a national of the country concerned, shall not be considered discriminatory.

Conditions of Service and Tenure

11. The term of office of judges, their independence, security, adequate remuneration, conditions of service, pensions and the age of retirement shall be adequately secured by law.
12. Judges, whether appointed or elected, shall have guaranteed tenure until a mandatory retirement age or the expiry of their term of office, where such exists.
13. Promotion of judges, wherever such a system exists, should be based on objective factors, in particular ability, integrity and experience.
14. The assignment of cases to judges within the court to which they belong is an internal matter of judicial administration.

Professional Secrecy and Immunity

15. The judiciary shall be bound by professional secrecy with regard to their deliberations and to confidential information acquired in the course of their duties other than in public proceedings, and shall not be compelled to testify on such matters.

16. Without prejudice to any disciplinary procedure or to any right of appeal or to compensation from the State, in accordance with national law, judges should enjoy personal immunity from civil suits for monetary damages for improper acts or omissions in the exercise of their judicial functions.

Discipline, Suspension and Removal

17. A charge or complaint made against a judge in his/her judicial and professional capacity shall be processed expeditiously and fairly under an appropriate procedure. The judge shall have the right to a fair hearing. The examination of the matter at its initial stage shall be kept confidential, unless otherwise requested by the judge.
18. Judges shall be subject to suspension or removal only for reasons of incapacity or behaviour that renders them unfit to discharge their duties.
19. All disciplinary, suspension or removal proceedings shall be determined in accordance with established standards of judicial conduct.
20. Decisions in disciplinary, suspension or removal proceedings should be subject to an independent review. This principle may not apply to the decisions of the highest court and those of the legislature in impeachment or similar proceedings.

4 Conclusion

The UN Basic Principles and Guidelines provide a useful starting point and a reference framework to guide judges and lawyers worldwide on the importance of safeguarding the independence of the judiciary and the legal profession. There are calls for the Basic Principles and Guidelines to be updated and modernized in the light of contemporary challenges. This updating and modernization has become urgent.

7 Universally-binding Human Rights Norms

1 Introduction

The World Conference on Human Rights held in Vienna in 1993 famously declared that "The universal nature of these rights and freedoms is beyond question."[1] The UN's Millennium Declaration resolved "... to respect fully and uphold the Universal Declaration of Human Rights; to strive for the full protection and promotion in all our countries of civil, political, economic, social and cultural rights for all."[2]

The story of human history has been one of human societies cross-fertilizing and learning from one another, converging toward a great synthesis around binding international human rights norms. Viewed from this perspective, the universality of rights has been authoritatively affirmed in the international community, and there is a formal consensus on universality.

The universality of human rights must be vigorously upheld. It rests on the idea that there is a minimum body of basic human rights that belongs to every human being regardless of his or her country of origin or philosophical, religious, or other beliefs. Regional or national charters may add to the universal body of human rights but may not detract from them.

The validity of the universality of human rights is not lessened by the fact that, in practice, human rights are violated in many parts of the world. But rights exist even if they are breached, and the challenge is to work for their implementation and protection. This chapter discusses universality as an idea, a goal, a normative concept, its democratic test, the basis of universality, and problems of implementation.

2 Universality as an Idea

The concept of human rights has developed over the centuries and has roots in all of the major world religions and philosophies. In turn, these principles have been codified in international legal instruments, namely the Universal Declaration of Human Rights (UDHR). Since its launch in 1948, the UDHR has been re-endorsed in international and regional treaties and in authoritative policy pronouncements by governments and people in Africa, the Americas, Asia, and Europe. This certainly underscores the universality of human rights.

---

1 Vienna Declaration, para. 1.

2 Millennium Declaration, para. 25.

Some years ago, the late Senator José Diokno of the Philippines, delivering the Amnesty International lecture[3], summarily dispatched spurious arguments about cultural diversity that diminished universality:

> Two justifications for authoritarianism in Asian developing countries are currently fashionable... One is that Asian societies are authoritarian and paternalistic and so need governments that are also authoritarian and paternalistic; that Asia's hungry masses are too concerned with filling their stomachs to concern themselves with civil liberties and political freedoms; that the Asian conception of freedom differs from that of the West; that, in short, Asians are not fit for human rights.
>
> Another is that developing countries must sacrifice freedom temporarily to achieve the rapid economic development that their exploding populations and rising expectations demand; in short, that governments must be authoritarian to promote development.
>
> Well, the first justification is racist nonsense. And I will say no more than that. The second is a lie: authoritarianism is not needed for development; what it is needed for is to maintain the status quo.
>
> Regardless... of what dictators and social scientists may say, we Asians know that the loss of freedom does not lead to a better life. On the contrary, we know that life cannot become better—it cannot even be good—unless people are free.

3 Universality as a Goal

If human beings have so many things in common, is it strange to want to preserve these shared characteristics and to reach out in mutual support and cooperation? Can we protect the environment or keep the air clean unless we do so together? Is it wrong to say that every human being should have an equal opportunity to develop his or her potential? Is universality then not valid as a goal for shared aspirations?

The idea that all human beings, in the first quarter of the twenty-first century, possess, as part of their birthright, a core of inalienable rights is not disputed by most countries of the world. What is sometimes debated is the content of particular rights and the need for change. This is a legitimate debate. The international human rights treaties inspired by the UDHR contain amendment procedures that could deal with claims for modernization

3 1978 Sean MacBride Human Rights Lecture delivered by Jose Diokno, former senator of the Republic of the Philippines. Amnesty International, 1978.

or updating. The UDHR, however, stands on its own as a historic, inspirational document. The universality of core human rights is quite compatible with cultural diversity, and the argument of cultural diversity should not challenge the core universal human rights but, rather, might influence the mode and manner of their application in particular societies. One can, for example, proclaim freedom of religion or belief, while leaving it to each person to choose a religion or belief. The notion of good faith in applying universal human rights norms comes into the picture here.

The existence of duties does not negate the universality of human rights. Rather, as is explicitly recognized in Article 29 of the UDHR, everyone has duties to his or her community. That same article further states that one's rights may be subject only to such limitations as are determined by law in the exercise of rights and freedoms. Such limitations may only be for the purpose of securing due recognition and respect for the rights and freedoms of others and of meeting the requirements of morality, public order, and general welfare.

4 Universality as a Normative Concept

In the history of the international community, has it not been found necessary to postulate universal norms of conduct? And have the norms not been useful? Is not the very notion of international law grounded in the concept of a law applicable to all communities – at least in respect of imperative norms of public policy *(jus cogens)* and international customary law? Would order be possible in the international community without a system of norms of universal applicability and validity? The answer can only be in the negative. That being the case, is it not entirely natural and proper that the stock of norms of international law would also include norms of universal human rights?

By the very act of joining the organization, all UN Member States commit to the principle of universality contained in the Charter and the UDHR. The commitment to universality is itself universal. When the Commission on Human Rights began drafting the UDHR in 1947, Charles Malik of Lebanon urged that the Commission base itself on the following four principles:

(a) The human person is more important than the racial, national, or other group to which he may belong;
(b) The human person's most sacred and inviolable possessions are in his mind and his conscience, enabling him to perceive the truth, choose freely, and to exist;
(c) Any social pressure on the part of the state, religion, or race involving the automatic consent of the human person is reprehensible;

(d) The social group to which the individual belongs may, like the human person himself, be wrong or right. The person alone is the judge.

The spirit animating the drafting committee members is inspiring to read, even several decades later. At an early drafting session, René Cassin proposed that two or three fundamental principles be incorporated in the outline:

(a) The unity of the human race or family;
(b) The idea that every human being has a right to be treated like every other human being;
(c) The concept of solidarity and fraternity among men.

Hernán Santa Cruz of Chile opined that the drafting committee must draw up a charter of human rights, giving it not only legal but real human content. He further suggested that this charter should be a spiritual guide for humanity, enumerating the rights that must be respected everywhere.

The UDHR's opening article was significantly influenced by Asia. During the second session of the drafting committee, on 5 December 1947, Carlos Romulo of the Philippines proposed to redraft Article 1 as discussed in the first session in June 1947 on the basis of René Cassin's draft proposal. In response, the chairperson invited the French and Philippine representatives to submit a new text of the article. At the ninth meeting of the drafting committee, on 10 December 1947, Romulo proposed the following text: "All men are brothers. Being endowed by nature with reason and conscience, they are born free and possess equal dignity and rights."

Following further discussion, the following text proposed by the Philippines and France was adopted: "All men are born free and equal in dignity and rights. They are endowed with reason and conscience and should act towards one another like brothers." With some subsequent polishing, the following is what was adopted as the UDHR's opening article: "All human beings are born free and equal in dignity and rights. They are endowed with reason and conscience and should act towards one another in a spirit of brotherhood."

The Egyptian representative, Osman Obeid, made the following stirring plea for justice for the peoples of the world: "The principles of human rights should be set forth in clear terms. The peoples of the world would greet with enthusiasm the first action taken by the United Nations to enforce redressment of wrongs."

Representatives from Africa, Asia, the Americas, and Europe thus influenced the drafting of the UDHR. In the drafting process, detailed draft declarations were submitted by Chile, Cuba, and Panama. In compiling materials from all over the globe to aid in drafting the declaration, the secretariat drew on the constitutions and legislation of 55 countries from Africa, Asia,

Latin America, and Eastern Europe. Only 14 were from Western countries.

Developing countries also were actively involved. The Philippines proposed an article stating that everyone had the right to participate in their government, both directly or indirectly, through elections that are periodic, free, and conducted by secret ballot. The Panamanian representative proposed an article declaring that the state has a duty to maintain comprehensive arrangements to promote health, prevent sickness and accident, and provide medical care and compensation for the loss of livelihood.

Malik argued that social and economic rights, and the problem of discrimination, were very important and should form part of the instrument. P C. Chang of China called for a document that would accord with the spirit and atmosphere of the post-war era and argued that the document should reflect freedom from want. India tabled a draft declaration that included the following statement: "Every human being has the right of equality, without distinction of race, sex, language, religion, nationality or political belief."

This is a mere sampling of the defining contributions of the representatives from Africa, Asia, and Latin America in drafting the UDHR. At the World Conference on Human Rights in 1993, the representatives, assembled from around the world, reaffirmed the universality of human rights in the most emphatic terms.

The UDHR has inspired regional instruments to protect human rights throughout the globe, all of which have reaffirmed its precepts. This may be seen in the constitution of the OAU (now the African Union), the African Charter on Human and People's Rights, the Arab Charter on Human Rights, the Cairo Islamic Declaration on Human Rights, the ASEAN Human Rights Declaration, the LAWASIA Statement of Basic Principles of Human Rights, the American Convention on Human Rights, and the European Convention on Human Rights. These endorsements of the UDHR bear witness to its universal status.

5 The Democratic Test of Universality

There is an irrefutable democratic test that confirms the concept of the universality of rights. It is a simple matter. Just ask any human being: Would you like to live or be killed arbitrarily? Would you like to be tortured or enslaved? Would you like to live free or be in prison? Would you like to be in bondage? Would you like to have a say in how you are governed? The democratic test of universality is the basis for its strongest affirmation.

6 The Bases of Universality

The bases of the universality of human rights are: (1) all human beings claim their inherent human rights; (2) the common humanity of all human beings and the inherency of rights; (3) the formal affirmation and reaffirmation of human rights in consensual processes of authoritative decision-making bodies such as the GA and world conferences on human rights.

There may, indeed, be discussion about whether every internationally proclaimed human right is universal, or if global consensus is lacking regarding a particular asserted right. There is, for example, a lively debate about the right to change one's religion or belief. This right was included in the UDHR but not in the International Covenant on Civil and Political Rights and was finessed in the 1992 Declaration on Freedom of Religion or Belief. Where a particular human right is contested by one or more government or group, the matter must be assessed by referring to the tests of inherency and consensus.

When a right is contested, recourse may be had to the principle of inherency, namely that one should enjoy certain rights from the very nature of one's common humanity. The example of the right to change one's religion or belief may be cited. One can understand religions or laws prohibiting religious proselytizing or forbidding campaigns to convince people to change religions. But if an individual decides to change her or his religion or belief, how can this be forbidden by any religion or law? The universality of the right to change one's religion or belief would therefore rest in the principle of inherency.

There are repeated instances of the reaffirmation of consensus over the universality of human rights in authoritative fora of the international community such as the Vienna World Conference on Human Rights, the Millennium Declaration, and the outcome document of the Summit of World Leaders in 2005.

The Vienna Conference reaffirmed all states' solemn commitment to fulfill their obligations to promote universal respect for, observance of, and protection of all human rights and fundamental freedoms in accordance with the UN Charter, other instruments relating to human rights, and international law. In ringing terms, it proclaimed that: "The universal nature of these rights and freedoms is beyond question."

The Millennium Declaration reaffirmed the UN's commitment to the Charter's purposes and principles, "which have proved timeless and universal. Indeed, their relevance and capacity to inspire have increased, as nations and peoples have become increasingly interconnected and interdependent." It pledged: "We resolve... to respect fully and uphold the Universal Declaration of Human Rights; to strive for the full protection and promotion in all our countries of civil, political, economic, social and cultural rights for all."

The UNGA considered certain fundamental values essential to international relations in the twenty-first century. These included freedom, equality, solidarity, tolerance, respect for nature, and shared responsibility.

The Summit of World Leaders in 2005 reaffirmed the centrality of human rights in the UN's work and endorsed the responsibility to protect. The world leaders declared their readiness to refer genocide, ethnic cleansing, crimes against humanity, and war crimes to the UNSC.

7 Challenges of Implementation

It has been argued that the universality of human rights is belied by the fact that these rights are not respected in practice or are grossly violated in large parts of the world. Lack of implementation is certainly a feature of our contemporary world. So are gross violations of human rights. But this is not an argument against universality. In national legal systems, the validity of laws is not belied by the fact that many are breached on the ground. This is an issue of law and order and protection.

An individual's rights are not nullified because they are not respected or are violated. This is a challenge of universal implementation and protection that the entire international human rights movement is striving to address.

To reiterate, there is a simple test of universality. If any human being were asked whether she or he would like to be free from arbitrary and summary execution, torture, arbitrary arrest and detention, enforced or involuntary disappearance, and persecution on grounds of religion or belief, there can be no doubt that every human being would answer in the positive. From this, we may conclude that there is a basic set of fundamental human rights that all human beings would claim, affirm, and defend.

8 Conclusion

This chapter has sought to discuss the historical and philosophical groundings of universal human rights. In Appendix I below, we provide a Recapitulation of Core Universally-binding Human Rights Norms.

8 Governmental Obligations to 'Prevent', 'Respect', 'Protect', 'Ensure', 'Fulfil', 'Guarantee' in International Law

1 Introduction

Universally-binding human rights norms may require Governments to prevent violations of human rights, to protect human rights, to respect human rights, to fulfil human rights, to ensure human rights, or to guarantee human rights. Each of these terms has legal significance and, in this chapter, we look at some of their meanings.

In the Velásquez Rodriguez Case (1988), the Inter-American Court of Human Rights[1] dealt with Article 1 (1) of the American Convention on Human Rights which provides as follows: "1. The States Parties to this Convention undertake to respect the rights and freedoms recognized herein and to ensure to all persons subject to their jurisdiction the free and full exercise of those rights and freedoms, without any discrimination..." The Court held that according to Article 1(1), any exercise of public power that violates the rights recognized by the Convention is illegal. Whenever a State organ, official or public entity violates one of those rights, this constitutes a failure of the duty to respect the rights and freedoms set forth in the Convention. This conclusion was independent of whether the organ or official had contravened provisions of internal law or overstepped the limits of his authority; under international law a State was responsible for the acts of its agents undertaken in their official capacity and for their omissions, even when those agents acted outside the sphere of their authority or violated internal law.[2]

Furthermore, an illegal act which violated human rights and which was initially not directly imputable to a State (for example, because it was the act of a private person or because the person responsible had not been identified) could lead to international responsibility of the State, not because of the act itself, but because of the lack of diligence to prevent the violation or to respond to it as required by the Convention.[3] What was decisive was whether a violation of the rights recognized by the Convention had occurred with the support or the acquiescence of the government, or

1 4 Inter-Am. Ct. H.R. (ser C).
2 *Ibid.*, para. 170.
3 *Ibid.*, para. 172.

whether the State had allowed the act to take place without taking measures to prevent it or to punish those responsible.[4]

The State has, the Court continued, the legal duty to take reasonable steps to prevent human rights violations and to use the means at its disposal to carry out a serious investigation of violations committed within its jurisdiction, to identify those responsible, to impose the appropriate punishment and to ensure the victim adequate compensation.

2 The Concept of Prevention

The primary responsibility for the prevention of violations of human rights lies with the national protection system of each State. In the Velásquez Rodriguez Case (1988), the Inter-American Court of Human Rights had a superb discussion of the duty of Governments to prevent human rights violations. The State has, the Court declared, the legal duty to take reasonable steps to prevent human rights violations and to use the means at its disposal to carry out a serious investigation of violations committed within its jurisdiction, to identify those responsible, to impose the appropriate punishment and to ensure the victim adequate compensation.[5]

The duty to prevent, the Court continued, includes all those means of a legal, political, administrative and cultural nature that promote the protection of human rights and ensure that any violations are considered and treated as illegal acts, which, as such, may lead to the punishment of those responsible and the obligation to indemnify the victims for damages. The Court clarified, however, that while the State is obligated to prevent human rights abuses, the existence of a particular violation did not, in itself, prove the failure to take preventive measures. On the other hand, subjecting a person to official, repressive bodies that practiced torture and assassination with impunity was itself a breach of the duty to prevent violations of the rights to life and physical integrity of the person, even if that particular person was not tortured or assassinated, or if those facts could not be proven in a concrete case.[6]

Human rights treaty bodies have given solid guidance on the necessity for preventive measures against violations of human rights. We look at some of these next.

---

4 *Ibid.*, para. 173.

5 Inter-American Court of Human Rights, The Case of Velásquez-Rodríguez v. Honduras, 4 Inter-Am. Ct. H.R. (ser. C), para. 174.

6 *Ibid.*, para. 175.

2.1 *The Prevention of Torture*

In its General Comment No. 2 (2007), the Committee Against Torture commented at length on the content of the obligation to take effective measures to prevent torture. For a start, States parties must make the offence of torture punishable as an offence under its criminal law, at a minimum, with the elements of torture as defined in Article 1 of the Convention against Torture, and the requirements of article 4. The Committee warned that serious discrepancies between the Convention's definition and that incorporated into domestic law create actual or potential loopholes for impunity. It was essential to investigate and establish the responsibility of persons in the chain of command as well as that of the direct perpetrator(s).

By defining the offence of torture as distinct from common assault or other crimes, the Committee considered that States parties will directly advance the Convention's overarching aim of preventing torture and ill-treatment. Naming and defining this crime will promote the Convention's aim, *inter alia,* by alerting everyone, including perpetrators, victims and the public, to the special gravity of the crime of torture. Codifying the crime would also emphasize the need for appropriate punishment that takes into account the gravity of the offence; strengthen the deterrent effect of the prohibition itself; enhance the ability of responsible officials to track the specific crime of torture; and enable and empower the public to monitor and, when required, to challenge State action as well as State inaction that violates the Convention.

Preventive measures identified by the Committee included: maintaining an official register of detainees, the right of detainees to be informed of their rights, the right promptly to receive independent legal assistance, independent medical assistance, and to contact relatives, the need to establish impartial mechanism for inspecting and visiting places of detention and confinement, and the availability to detainees and persons at risk of torture and ill-treatment of judicial and other remedies that would allow them to have their complaints promptly and impartially examined, to defend their rights, and to challenge the legality of their detention or treatment. As new methods of prevention (e.g. videotaping all interrogations, utilizing investigative procedures such as the Istanbul Protocol of 1999, or new approaches to public education or the protection of minors) are discovered, tested and found effective, Article 2 of the Convention provided authority to build upon the remaining articles and to expand the scope of measures required to prevent torture.[7]

We discuss the prevention of torture in more detail later in this chapter.

---

7 HRI/GEN/1/Rev.9, p. 379.

2.1 *Preventing Racial Discrimination in the Administration and Functioning of the Criminal Justice System*

In its General Recommendation XXXI (2005), the Committee on the Elimination of Racial Discrimination provided guidance on strategies needed to prevent racial discrimination in the administration and functioning of the criminal justice system. States parties, it counselled, should pursue national strategies the objectives of which include the following:

(a) To eliminate laws that have an impact in terms of racial discrimination, particularly those which target certain groups indirectly by penalizing acts which can be committed only by persons belonging to such groups, or laws that apply only to non-nationals without legitimate grounds or which do not respect the principle of proportionality;

(b) To develop, through appropriate education programmes, training in respect for human rights, tolerance and friendship among racial or ethnic groups, as well as sensitization to intercultural relations, for law enforcement officials: police personnel, persons working in the system of justice, prison institutions, psychiatric establishments, social and medical services, etc;

(c) To foster dialogue and cooperation between the police and judicial authorities and the representatives of relevant groups in order to combat prejudice and create a relationship of trust;

(d) To promote proper representation of persons belonging to racial and ethnic groups in the police and the system of justice;

(e) To ensure respect for, and recognition of the traditional systems of justice of indigenous peoples, in conformity with international human rights law;

(f) To make the necessary changes to the prison regime for prisoners belonging to relevant groups so as to take into account their cultural and religious practices;

(g) To institute, in situations of mass population movements, the interim measures and arrangements necessary for the operation of the justice system in order to take account of the particularly vulnerable situation of displaced persons, in particular by setting up decentralized courts at the places where the displaced persons are staying or by organizing mobile courts.

(h) To set up, in post-conflict situations, plans for the reconstruction of the legal system and the re-establishment of the rule of law throughout the territory of the countries concerned by availing themselves, in particular, of the international technical assistance provided by the relevant United Nations entities;

(i) To implement national strategies or plans of action aimed at the elimination of structural discrimination. These long-term strategies should include specific objectives and actions as well as indicators against which progress can be measured. They should include, in particular, guidelines for prevention, recording, investigation and prosecution of racist or xenophobic incidents, assessment of the level of satisfaction among all communities concerning their relations with the police and the system of justice, and recruitment and promotion in the judicial system of persons belonging to various racial or ethnic groups;

(j) To entrust an independent national institution with the task of tracking, monitoring and measuring progress made under the national plans of action and guidelines against racial discrimination, identifying undetected manifestations of racial discrimination and submitting recommendations and proposals for improvement.[8]

2.2 *Avoiding Discrimination against Women in National Strategies for the Prevention of AIDS*

In its General Recommendation No. 15 (1990), the Committee on the Elimination of Discrimination Against Women recommended that States parties intensify their efforts in disseminating information to increase public awareness of the risk of HIV infection and AIDS, especially in women and children, and of its effect on them; that programmes to combat AIDS should give special attention to the rights and needs of women and children, and to the factors relating to the reproductive role of women and their subordinate position in some societies which make them especially vulnerable to HIV infection; that States parties ensure the active participation of women in primary health and take measures to enhance their role as care providers, health workers and educators in the prevention of infection with HIV; and that all States parties include in their reports under Article 12 of the Convention on the Elimination of All Forms of Discrimination against Women information on the effects of AIDS on the situation of women and on the action taken to cater to the needs of those women who are infected and to prevent specific discrimination against women in response to AIDS.[9]

---

8 *Ibid.*, pp. 309–310.

9 *Ibid.*, pp. 327–328.

2.3 *Preventing Deprivation of Liberty of Children and Treatment in Cases Thereof*

In General Comment No. 6, which dealt with the treatment of unaccompanied and separated children outside their country of origin, the Committee on the Rights of the Child provided guidance on a variety of measures for the prevention of trafficking and of sexual and other forms of exploitation, abuse and violence; prevention of military recruitment and protection against effects of war; and prevention of deprivation of liberty and treatment in cases thereof. In application of Article 37 of the Convention on the Rights of the Child, and in accordance with the principle of the best interests of the child, the Committee counselled, unaccompanied or separated children should not, as a general rule, be detained. Detention could not be justified solely on the basis of the child being unaccompanied or separated, or on their migratory or residence status, or lack thereof. In the exceptional case of detention, conditions of detention must be governed by the best interests of the child.[10]

2.4 *More on the Prevention of Torture*

Article 1 of the Convention against Torture and Other Cruel, Inhuman or Degrading Treatment or Punishment[11]defines 'torture' as any act by which severe pain or suffering, whether physical or mental, is intentionally inflicted on a person for such purposes as obtaining from him or a third person information or a confession, punishing him for an act he or a third person has committed or is suspected of having committed, or intimidating or coercing him or a third person, or for any reason based on discrimination of any kind, when such pain or suffering is inflicted by or at the instigation of or with the consent or acquiescence of a public official or other person acting in an official capacity. It does not include pain or suffering arising only from, inherent in or incidental to lawful sanctions. Article 2 requires each State Party to take effective legislative, administrative, judicial or other measures to prevent acts of torture in any territory under its jurisdiction. No exceptional circumstances whatsoever, whether a state of war or a threat of war, internal political instability or any other public emergency, may be invoked as a justification of torture. An order from a superior officer or a public authority may not be invoked as a justification of torture.

Under Article 3, no State Party shall expel, return (*refouler*) or extradite

---

10 *Ibid.*, pp. 455–459.

11 Adopted and opened for signature, ratification and accession by General Assembly Resolution 39/46 of 10 December 1984. Entry into force 26 June 1987, in accordance with Article 27 (1). 1465 UNTS 85.

a person to another State where there are substantial grounds for believing that he would be in danger of being subjected to torture. For the purpose of determining whether there are such grounds, the competent authorities shall take into account all relevant considerations including, where applicable, the existence in the State concerned of a consistent pattern of gross, flagrant or mass violations of human rights.

Article 4 requires that each State Party shall ensure that all acts of torture are offences under its criminal law. The same shall apply to an attempt to commit torture and to an act by any person which constitutes complicity or participation in torture. 2. Each State Party shall make these offences punishable by appropriate penalties which take into account their grave nature. Furthermore, under Article 5, each State Party shall take such measures as may be necessary to establish its jurisdiction over the offences referred to in Article 4 in the following cases: (a) When the offences are committed in any territory under its jurisdiction or on board a ship or aircraft registered in that State; (b) When the alleged offender is a national of that State; (c) When the victim is a national of that State if that State considers it appropriate.

Each State Party shall likewise take such measures as may be necessary to establish its jurisdiction over such offences in cases where the alleged offender is present in any territory under its jurisdiction and it does not extradite him pursuant to article 8 to any of the States mentioned in paragraph I of this article.

Furthermore, each State Party shall keep under systematic review interrogation rules, instructions, methods and practices as well as arrangements for the custody and treatment of persons subjected to any form of arrest, detention or imprisonment in any territory under its jurisdiction, with a view to preventing any cases of torture.

Under Article 12 each State Party shall ensure that its competent authorities proceed to a prompt and impartial investigation, wherever there is reasonable ground to believe that an act of torture has been committed in any territory under its jurisdiction.

Article 13 provides that each State Party shall ensure that any individual who alleges he has been subjected to torture in any territory under its jurisdiction has the right to complain to, and to have his case promptly and impartially examined by its competent authorities. Steps shall be taken to ensure that the complainant and witnesses are protected against all ill-treatment or intimidation as a consequence of his complaint or any evidence given.

Each State Party, under Article 14, shall ensure in its legal system that the victim of an act of torture obtains redress and has an enforceable right to fair and adequate compensation, including the means for as full rehabilitation as possible. In the event of the death of the victim as a result of an act of torture, his dependants shall be entitled to compensation.

2. Nothing in this article shall affect any right of the victim or other persons to compensation which may exist under national law.

Article 15 requires that each State Party shall ensure that any statement which is established to have been made as a result of torture shall not be invoked as evidence in any proceedings, except against a person accused of torture as evidence that the statement was made.

Article 16 states that each State Party shall undertake to prevent in any territory under its jurisdiction other acts of cruel, inhuman or degrading treatment or punishment which do not amount to torture as defined in article I, when such acts are committed by or at the instigation of, or with the consent or acquiescence of a public official or other person acting in an official capacity. In particular, the obligations contained in articles 10, 11, 12 and 13 shall apply with the substitution for references to torture of references to other forms of cruel, inhuman or degrading treatment or punishment. The provisions of the Convention are without prejudice to the provisions of any other international instrument or national law which prohibits cruel, inhuman or degrading treatment or punishment or which relates to extradition or expulsion.

Under Article 17 there is established a Committee against Torture consisting of ten experts of high moral standing and recognized competence in the field of human rights, who serve in their personal capacity. If the Committee receives reliable information which appears to it to contain well-founded indications that torture is being systematically practised in the territory of a State Party, the Committee shall, under Article 20, invite that State Party to co-operate in the examination of the information and to this end to submit observations with regard to the information concerned. Taking into account any observations which may have been submitted by the State Party concerned, as well as any other relevant information available to it, the Committee may, if it decides that this is warranted, designate one or more of its members to make a confidential inquiry and to report to the Committee urgently. If an inquiry is made in accordance with this article, the Committee shall seek the co-operation of the State Party concerned. In agreement with that State Party, such an inquiry may include a visit to its territory.

After examining the findings of its member or members submitted in accordance with paragraph 2 of this article, the Committee shall transmit these findings to the State Party concerned together with any comments or suggestions which seem appropriate in view of the situation. All the proceedings of the Committee shall be confidential , and at all stages of the proceedings the co-operation of the State Party shall be sought. After such proceedings have been completed with regard to an inquiry made in accordance with paragraph 2, the Committee may, after consultations with the State Party concerned, decide to include a summary account of the results of the proceedings in its annual report made in accordance with Article 24.

Article 21 provides that a State Party to the Convention may at any time declare that it recognizes the competence of the Committee to receive and consider communications to the effect that a State Party claims that another State Party is not fulfilling its obligations under the Convention. Such communications may be received and considered according to the procedures laid down in this article only if submitted by a State Party which has made a declaration recognizing in regard to itself the competence of the Committee. No communication shall be dealt with by the Committee under this article if it concerns a State Party which has not made such a declaration. Communications received under this article shall be dealt with in accordance with the following procedure:

(a) If a State Party considers that another State Party is not giving effect to the provisions of this Convention, it may, by written communication, bring the matter to the attention of that State Party. Within three months after the receipt of the communication the receiving State shall afford the State which sent the communication an explanation or any other statement in writing clarifying the matter, which should include, to the extent possible and pertinent, reference to domestic procedures and remedies taken, pending or available in the matter;

(b) If the matter is not adjusted to the satisfaction of both States Parties concerned within six months after the receipt by the receiving State of the initial communication, either State shall have the right to refer the matter to the Committee, by notice given to the Committee and to the other State;

(c) The Committee shall deal with a matter referred to it under this article only after it has ascertained that all domestic remedies have been invoked and exhausted in the matter, in conformity with the generally recognized principles of international law. This shall not be the rule where the application of the remedies is unreasonably prolonged or is unlikely to bring effective relief to the person who is the victim of the violation of this Convention;

(d) The Committee shall hold closed meetings when examining communications under this article;

(e) Subject to the provisions of subparagraph (c), the Committee shall make available its good offices to the States Parties concerned with a view to a friendly solution of the matter on the basis of respect for the obligations provided for in this Convention. For this purpose, the Committee may, when appropriate, set up an ad hoc conciliation commission;

(f) In any matter referred to it under this article, the Committee may call upon the States Parties concerned, referred to in subparagraph (b), to supply any relevant information;

(g) The States Parties concerned, referred to in subparagraph (b), shall have the right to be represented when the matter is being considered by the Committee and to make submissions orally and/or in writing;

(h) The Committee shall, within twelve months after the date of receipt of notice under subparagraph (b), submit a report: (i) If a solution within the terms of subparagraph (e) is reached, the Committee shall confine its report to a brief statement of the facts and of the solution reached; (ii) If a solution within the terms of subparagraph (e) is not reached, the Committee shall confine its report to a brief statement of the facts; the written submissions and record of the oral submissions made by the States Parties concerned shall be attached to the report. In every matter, the report shall be communicated to the States Parties concerned.

Under Article 22, a State Party to the Convention may at any time declare under this article that it recognizes the competence of the Committee to receive and consider communications from or on behalf of individuals subject to its jurisdiction who claim to be victims of a violation by a State Party of the provisions of the Convention. No communication shall be received by the Committee if it concerns a State Party which has not made such a declaration. The Committee is required to bring any communications submitted to it under this article to the attention of the State Party to this Convention which has made a declaration under paragraph I and is alleged to be violating any provisions of the Convention. Within six months, the receiving State shall submit to the Committee written explanations or statements clarifying the matter and the remedy, if any, that may have been taken by that State.

The Committee considers communications received under this article in the light of all information made available to it by or on behalf of the individual and by the State Party concerned.

2.4.1 Optional Protocol to the Convention against Torture and other Cruel, Inhuman or Degrading Treatment or Punishment[12]

This Protocol recalls that the effective prevention of torture and other cruel, inhuman or degrading treatment or punishment requires education and a combination of various legislative, administrative, judicial and other measures, and that the World Conference on Human Rights had firmly declared that efforts to eradicate torture should first and foremost be concentrated on prevention and had called for the adoption of an optional protocol to the Convention, intended to establish a preventive system of regular visits to places of detention,

The objective of the Protocol, as stated in Article 1, is to establish a system of regular visits undertaken by independent international and national bodies to places where people are deprived of their liberty, in order to prevent torture and other cruel, inhuman or degrading treatment or punishment. Article 2 provides for the establishment of a Subcommittee on Prevention of Torture and Other Cruel, Inhuman or Degrading Treatment or Punishment of the Committee against Torture.

The Subcommittee on Prevention is required to carry out its work within the framework of the Charter of the United Nations and to be guided by the Purposes and Principles thereof, as well as the norms of the United Nations concerning the treatment of people deprived of their liberty. The Subcommittee on Prevention shall be guided by the principles of confidentiality, impartiality, non-selectivity, universality and objectivity.

Each State Party, under Article 3, shall set up, designate or maintain at the domestic level one or several visiting bodies for the prevention of torture and other cruel, inhuman or degrading treatment or punishment (hereinafter referred to as the national preventive mechanism). Furthermore, in accordance with Article 4, each State Party shall allow visits by the mechanisms referred to in articles 2 and 3 to any place under its jurisdiction and control where persons are or may be deprived of their liberty, either by virtue of an order given by a public authority or at its instigation or with its consent or acquiescence (places of detention). These visits shall be undertaken with a view to strengthening, if necessary, the protection of these persons against torture and other cruel, inhuman or degrading treatment or punishment. Deprivation of liberty means any form of detention or imprisonment or the placement of a person in a public or private custodial setting which that person is not permitted to leave at will by order of

12 Adopted on 18 December 2002 at the fifty-seventh session of the General Assembly of the United Nations by resolution A/RES/57/199. Entered into force on 22 June 2006. 2375 UNTS 237.

any judicial, administrative or other authority.

The Subcommittee on Prevention, as specified in Article 5, consists consist of ten members. After the fiftieth ratification of or accession to the Protocol, the number of the members of the Subcommittee on Prevention shall increase to twenty-five. The members of the Subcommittee on Prevention shall be chosen from among persons of high moral character, having proven professional experience in the field of the administration of justice, in particular criminal law, prison or police administration, or in the various fields relevant to the treatment of persons deprived of their liberty.

Under Article 11, The Subcommittee on Prevention shall:

(a) Visit the places referred to in Article 4 and make recommendations to States Parties concerning the protection of persons deprived of their liberty against torture and other cruel, inhuman or degrading treatment or punishment;

(b) In regard to the national preventive mechanisms: (i) Advise and assist States Parties, when necessary, in their establishment; (ii) Maintain direct, and if necessary confidential, contact with the national preventive mechanisms and offer them training and technical assistance with a view to strengthening their capacities; (iii) Advise and assist them in the evaluation of the needs and the means necessary to strengthen the protection of persons deprived of their liberty against torture and other cruel, inhuman or degrading treatment or punishment;(iv) Make recommendations and observations to the States Parties with a view to strengthening the capacity and the mandate of the national preventive mechanisms for the prevention of torture and other cruel, inhuman or degrading treatment or punishment;

(c) Cooperate, for the prevention of torture in general, with the relevant United Nations organs and mechanisms as well as with the international, regional and national institutions or organizations working towards the strengthening of the protection of all persons against torture and other cruel, inhuman or degrading treatment or punishment.

In order to enable the Subcommittee on Prevention to comply with its mandate as laid down in Article 11, the States Parties undertake under Article 12:

(a) To receive the Subcommittee on Prevention in their territory and grant it access to the places of detention as defined in Article 4 of the present Protocol;

(b) To provide all relevant information the Subcommittee on Prevention may request to evaluate the needs and measures that should be adopted to strengthen the protection of persons deprived of their liberty against torture and other cruel, inhuman or degrading treatment or punishment;

(c) To encourage and facilitate contacts between the Subcommittee on Prevention and the national preventive mechanisms;

(d) To examine the recommendations of the Subcommittee on Prevention and enter into dialogue with it on possible implementation measures.

Article 13 calls for the Subcommittee on Prevention to establish, at first by lot, a programme of regular visits to the States Parties in order to fulfil its mandate as established in article 11. After consultations, the Subcommittee on Prevention shall notify the States Parties of its programme in order that they may, without delay, make the necessary practical arrangements for the visits to be conducted. The visits shall be conducted by at least two members of the Subcommittee on Prevention. These members may be accompanied, if needed, by experts of demonstrated professional experience and knowledge in the fields covered by the present Protocol who shall be selected from a roster of experts prepared on the basis of proposals made by the States Parties, the Office of the United Nations High Commissioner for Human Rights and the United Nations Centre for International Crime Prevention. In preparing the roster, the States Parties concerned shall propose no more than five national experts. The State Party concerned may oppose the inclusion of a specific expert in the visit, whereupon the Subcommittee on Prevention shall propose another expert. If the Subcommittee on Prevention considers it appropriate, it may propose a short follow-up visit after a regular visit.

In order to enable the Subcommittee on Prevention to fulfil its mandate, the States Parties undertake in Article 14 to the Protocol undertake to grant it:

(a) Unrestricted access to all information concerning the number of persons deprived of their liberty in places of detention as defined in article 4, as well as the number of places and their location;

(b) Unrestricted access to all information referring to the treatment of those persons as well as their conditions of detention;

(c) Subject to paragraph 2 below, unrestricted access to all places of detention and their installations and facilities;

(d) The opportunity to have private interviews with the persons deprived of their liberty without witnesses, either personally or with a translator if deemed necessary, as well as with any other person who the Subcommittee on Prevention believes may supply relevant information;

(e) The liberty to choose the places it wants to visit and the persons it wants to interview.

Objection to a visit to a particular place of detention may be made only on urgent and compelling grounds of national defence, public safety, natural disaster or serious disorder in the place to be visited that temporarily prevent the carrying out of such a visit. The existence of a declared state of emergency as such shall not be invoked by a State Party as a reason to object to a visit.

As provided for in Article 15, no authority or official shall order, apply, permit or tolerate any sanction against any person or organization for having communicated to the Subcommittee on Prevention or to its delegates any information, whether true or false, and no such person or organization shall be otherwise prejudiced in any way.

Article 16 provides that the Subcommittee on Prevention shall communicate its recommendations and observations confidentially to the State Party and, if relevant, to the national preventive mechanism. The Subcommittee on Prevention shall publish its report, together with any comments of the State Party concerned, whenever requested to do so by that State Party. If the State Party makes part of the report public, the Subcommittee on Prevention may publish the report in whole or in part. However, no personal data shall be published without the express consent of the person concerned. The Subcommittee on Prevention shall present a public annual report on its activities to the Committee against Torture.

If the State Party refuses to cooperate with the Subcommittee on Prevention according to Articles 12 and 14, or to take steps to improve the situation in the light of the recommendations of the Subcommittee on Prevention, the Committee against Torture may, at the request of the Subcommittee on Prevention, decide, by a majority of its members, after the State Party has had an opportunity to make its views known, to make a public statement on the matter or to publish the report of the Subcommittee on Prevention.

Article 17 deals with national preventive mechanisms. It provides that each State Party shall maintain, designate or establish, at the latest one year after the entry into force of the present Protocol or of its ratification or accession, one or several independent national preventive mechanisms for the prevention of torture at the domestic level. Mechanisms established by decentralized units may be designated as national preventive mechanisms for the purposes of the present Protocol if they are in conformity with its provisions. The States Parties shall, under Article 18, guarantee the functional independence of the national preventive mechanisms as well as the independence of their personnel. The States Parties shall take the necessary measures to ensure that the experts of the national preventive mechanism have the required capabilities and professional knowledge. They shall strive for a gender balance and the adequate representation of ethnic and minority groups in the country. The States Parties undertake to make available the necessary resources for the functioning of the national preventive mechanisms. When establishing national preventive mechanisms, States Parties shall give due consideration to the UN Principles relating to the status of national institutions for the promotion and protection of human rights.

The national preventive mechanisms shall, in accordance with Article 19, be granted at a minimum the power:

(a) To regularly examine the treatment of the persons deprived of their liberty in places of detention as defined in article 4, with a view to strengthening, if necessary, their protection against torture and other cruel, inhuman or degrading treatment or punishment;
(b) To make recommendations to the relevant authorities with the aim of improving the treatment and the conditions of the persons deprived of their liberty and to prevent torture and other cruel, inhuman or degrading treatment or punishment, taking into consideration the relevant norms of the United Nations;
(c) To submit proposals and observations concerning existing or draft legislation.

In order to enable the national preventive mechanisms to fulfil their mandate, the States Parties to the Protocol undertake in Article 20 to grant them:

(a) Access to all information concerning the number of persons deprived of their liberty in places of detention as defined in article 4, as well as the number of places and their location;
(b) Access to all information referring to the treatment of those persons as well as their conditions of detention;
(c) Access to all places of detention and their installations and facilities;
(d) The opportunity to have private interviews with the persons deprived of their liberty without witnesses, either personally or with a translator if deemed necessary, as well as with any other person who the national preventive mechanism believes may supply relevant information;
(e) The liberty to choose the places they want to visit and the persons they want to interview;
(f) The right to have contacts with the Subcommittee on Prevention, to send it information and to meet with it.

Article 21 stipulates that no authority or official shall order, apply, permit or tolerate any sanction against any person or organization for having communicated to the national preventive mechanism any information, whether true or false, and no such person or organization shall be otherwise prejudiced in any way. Confidential information collected by the national preventive mechanism shall be privileged. No personal data shall be published without the express consent of the person concerned.

The competent authorities of the State Party concerned are required under Article 22 to examine the recommendations of the national preventive mechanism and enter into a dialogue with it on possible implementation measures.The States Parties to the present Protocol undertake in Article 23 to publish and disseminate the annual reports of the national preventive mechanisms.

2.4.2 European Convention for the Prevention of Torture and Inhuman or Degrading Treatment or Punishment[13]

The Member States of the Council of Europe which subscribe to the Convention affirm their conviction that the protection of persons deprived of their liberty against torture and inhuman or degrading treatment or punishment could be strengthened by non-judicial means of a preventive character based on visits. They therefore agreed in Article 1 to the establishment of a European Committee for the Prevention of Torture and Inhuman or Degrading Treatment or Punishment ("the Committee") which shall, by means of visits, examine the treatment of persons deprived of their liberty with a view to strengthening, if necessary, the protection of such persons from torture and from inhuman or degrading treatment or punishment.

Each Party agrees in Article 2 to permit visits, in accordance with the Convention, to any place within its jurisdiction where persons are deprived of their liberty by a public authority. In the application of this Convention, the Committee and the competent national authorities of the Party concerned shall, in accordance with Article 3, co-operate with each other.

The Committee, in accordance with Article 4, consists of a number of members equal to that of the Parties. The members of the Committee shall be chosen from among persons of high moral character, known for their competence in the field of human rights or having professional experience in the areas covered by this Convention.

Article 6 provides that the Committee shall meet in camera. A quorum shall be equal to the majority of its members. Under Article 7, the Committee shall organize visits to places referred to in Article 2. Apart from

13 Strasbourg, 26.XI.1987. Text amended according to the provisions of Protocols No. 1 (ETS No. 151) and No. 2 (ETS No. 152), which entered into force on 1 March 2002.

periodic visits, the Committee may organize such other visits as appear to it to be required in the circumstances. As a general rule, the visits shall be carried out by at least two members of the Committee. The Committee may, if it considers it necessary, be assisted by experts and interpreters.

The Committee is required, under Article 8, to notify the Government of the Party concerned of its intention to carry out a visit. After such notification, it may at any time visit any place referred to in Article 2. A Party shall provide the Committee with the following facilities to carry out its task:

a access to its territory and the right to travel without restriction;

b full information on the places where persons deprived of their liberty are being held;

c unlimited access to any place where persons are deprived of their liberty, including the right to move inside such places without restriction;

d other information available to the Party which is necessary for the Committee to carry out its task. In seeking such information, the Committee shall have regard to applicable rules of national law and professional ethics.

Furthermore, the Committee may interview in private persons deprived of their liberty. The Committee may communicate freely with any person whom it believes can supply relevant information. If necessary, the Committee may immediately communicate observations to the competent authorities of the Party concerned.

Article 9 states that in exceptional circumstances, the competent authorities of the Party concerned may make representations to the Committee against a visit at the time or to the particular place proposed by the Committee. Such representations may only be made on grounds of national defence, public safety, serious disorder in places where persons are deprived of their liberty, the medical condition of a person or that an urgent interrogation relating to a serious crime is in progress. Following such representations, the Committee and the Party shall immediately enter into consultations in order to clarify the situation and seek agreement on arrangements to enable the Committee to exercise its functions expeditiously. Such arrangements may include the transfer to another place of any person whom the Committee proposed to visit. Until the visit takes place, the Party shall provide information to the Committee about any person concerned.

After each visit, the Committee shall, in accordance with Article 10, draw up a report on the facts found during the visit, taking account of any observations which may have been submitted by the Party concerned. It shall transmit to the latter its report containing any recommendations it considers necessary. The Committee may consult with the Party with a view to suggesting, if necessary, improvements in the protection of persons deprived of their liberty. If the Party fails to co-operate or refuses to improve the situation in the light of the Committee's recommendations, the Committee may decide, after the Party has had an opportunity to make known its views, by a majority of two-thirds of its members to make a public statement on the matter.

The information gathered by the Committee in relation to a visit, its report and its consultations with the Party concerned shall, in accordance with Article 11, be confidential. The Committee shall publish its report, together with any comments of the Party concerned, whenever requested to do so by that Party. However, no personal data shall be published without the express consent of the person concerned.

Subject to the rules of confidentiality in Article 11, the Committee shall every year, in accordance with Article 12, submit to the Committee of Ministers a general report on its activities which shall be transmitted to the Consultative Assembly and to any non-member State of the Council of Europe which is a party to the Convention, and made public.

The members of the Committee, experts and other persons assisting the Committee are required, under Article 13, during and after their terms of office, to maintain the confidentiality of the facts or information of which they have become aware during the discharge of their functions.

Article 20 provides that the Committee shall not visit places which representatives or delegates of Protecting Powers or the International Committee of the Red Cross effectively visit on a regular basis by virtue of the Geneva Conventions of 12 August 1949 and the Additional Protocols of 8 June 1977 thereto.

Article 21 specifies that no reservation may be made in respect of the provisions of the Convention.

3 Human Rights in Times of Crises or Emergencies

The principle of international protection in situations of national declarations of emergency was superbly brought out by an ILO Commission of Inquiry in 1956. Responding to Greece's contention that it had proclaimed a state of emergency in accordance with its national law and that the Government was the sole judge of the need to proclaim a state of emergency, the Commission stated:

> The Commission understands perfectly the argument that conformity with the Constitution would make the Government in the eyes of

> Greek law the sole judge of the need to proclaim a state of emergency. But it is an accepted principle of international law that a State cannot rely on the terms of its national law, or otherwise invoke the concept of national sovereignty, to justify non-performance of an international obligation. Any doubt concerning the extent of such an obligation must be determined by exclusive reference to the relevant principles of international law, whether made express by the parties to a treaty or derived from another source of international law, in particular, international custom and general principles of law.[14]

The Commission added:

> All the main legal systems accept in some form the principle that pleas of justification on grounds such as self-defence are subject to legal review. If a plea of emergency is to be treated in international law as a legal concept there similarly has to be appraisal by an impartial authority at the international level. It is for this reason that international tribunals and supervisory organs, when seized of such a plea, have invariably made an independent determination of whether the circumstances justified the claim, and have not allowed the State concerned to be the sole judge of the issue.[15]

3.1 *The Core Provisions*

A governmental leader or officer contemplating the declaration of an emergency must first have regard to the governing provisions under relevant human rights treaties. The European Convention on Human Rights,[16] the International Covenant on Civil and Political Rights,[17] and the American Convention on Human Rights (hereafter the American Convention)[18] all have provisions on this topic. There is no matching provision in the

14 Report of the Commission Appointed under Article 26 of the Constitution of the ILO to Examine the Complaints concerning the Observance by Greece of the Freedom of Association and Protection of the Right to Organise Convention, 1948 (No.87) and of the Right to Organize and Collective Bargaining Convention, 1949 (No. 98), made by a number of delegates to the 52nd session of the International Labour Conference. ILO, Official Bulletin, Special Supplement, Vol. LIV. 1971, No. 2, pp. 25–26, paras. 102–112.

15 *Ibid.*

16 Rome, 1950. *Council of Europe Treaty Series 005*, Council of Europe, 1950.

17 New York, 1966. 999 UNTS 171.

18 Hereafter referred to as the American Convention on Human Rights (ACHR). San José (Costa Rica) 1969. 1144 UNTS 143.

African Charter on Human and Peoples' Rights[19] but there is solid case law of the African Commission on Human and Peoples' Rights. The African Commission has stated, for example:

> Governments should avoid restricting rights, and have special care with regard to those rights protected by constitutional and international human rights law. No situation justifies the wholesale violation of human rights. In fact, general restrictions on rights diminish public confidence in the rule of law and are often counter-productive...

According to Article 9(2) of the African Charter, dissemination of opinions may be restricted by law. This does not mean that national law can set aside the right to express and disseminate one's opinions, this would make the protection of the right to express one's opinions ineffective. To allow national law to have precedence over the international law of the Charter would defeat the purpose of the rights and freedoms enshrined in the Charter. International human rights standards must always prevail over contradictory national law. Any limitation on the rights of the Charter must be in conformity with the provisions of the Charter.

In contrast to other international human rights instruments, the African Charter does not contain a derogation clause. Therefore limitations on the rights and freedoms enshrined in the Charter cannot be justified by emergencies or special circumstances.

The only legitimate reasons for limitations to the rights and freedoms of the African Charter are found in Article 27(2), that the rights of the Charter "shall be exercised with due regard to the rights of others, collective security, morality and common interests..."

The reasons for possible limitations must be founded in a legitimate State interest and the evils of limitations of rights must be strictly proportionate with and absolutely necessary for the advantages which are to be obtained.

Even more important, a limitation may never have as a consequence that the right itself becomes illusory.[20]

---

19 Nairobi, 1981. 1520 UNTS 217.

20 Communications 105/93, 128/94 and 152/96, *Media Rights Agenda and Constitutional Rights Project v. Nigeria*, Media Rights Agenda and Constitutional Rights Project, Twelfth Activity Report 1998–1999, Annex V. See generally on Limitations, the Syracusa Principles and the Limberg Principles, annexed to this work.

3.2 *The European Convention on Human Rights (ECHR)*

Article 15 of the European Convention provides:

1 In time of war or other public emergency threatening the life of the nation any High Contracting Party may take measures derogating from its obligations under the Convention to the extent strictly required by the exigencies of the situation, provided that such measures are not inconsistent with its other obligations under international law.
2 No derogation from Article 2, except in respect of deaths resulting from lawful acts of war, or from Articles 3, 4 (paragraph 1) and 7 shall be made under this provision.
3 Any High Contracting Party availing itself of this right to derogation shall keep the Secretary-General of the Council of Europe fully informed of the measures which it has taken and the reasons therefore. It shall also inform the Secretary-General of the Council of Europe when such measures have ceased to operate and the provisions of the Convention are again being fully executed.

3.3 *The International Covenant on Civil and Political Rights (ICCPR)*

Article 4 of the International Covenant on Civil and Political Rights provides:

1 In time of pubic emergency which threatens the life of the nation and the existence of which is officially proclaimed, the States Parties to the present Convention may take measures derogating from their obligations under the present Covenant to the extent strictly required by the exigencies of the situation, provided that such measures are not inconsistent with their other obligations under international law and do not involve discrimination solely on the ground of race, colour, sex, language, religion or social origin.
2 No derogation from articles 6, 7, 8 (paragraphs 1 and 2), 11, 15, 16 and 18 may be made under this provision.
3 Any State Party to the present Covenant availing itself of the right of derogation shall immediately inform the other States parties to the present covenant, through the intermediary of the Secretary-General of the United Nations, of the provisions from which it has derogated and of the reasons by which it was actuated. A

further communication shall be made, through the same intermediary, on the date on which it terminates such derogations.

3.4 *The American Convention on Human Rights (ACHR)*

Article 27 of the American Convention provides:

1 In time of war, public danger, or other emergency that threatens the independence or security of a State Party, it may take measures derogating from its obligations under the present Convention to the extent and for the period of time strictly required by the exigencies of the situation, provided that such measures are not inconsistent with its other obligations under international law and do not involve discrimination on the grounds of race, colour, sex, language, religion, or social origin.

2 The foregoing provision does not authorize any suspension of the following articles: Article 3 (Right to Juridical Personality), Article 3 (Right to Life), Article 5 (Right to Humane Treatment), Article 6 (Freedom from Slavery), Article 9 (Freedom from *Ex Post Facto* Laws), Article 12 (Freedom of Conscience and Religion), Article 17 (Rights of the Family), Article 18 (Right to a Name), Article 19 (Rights of the Child), Article 20 (Right to Nationality), and Article 23 (Right to Participate in Government), or of the judicial guarantees essential for the protection of such rights.

3 Any State Party availing itself of the right of suspension shall immediately inform the other

4 States Parties, through the Secretary-General of the Organization of American States, of the provision the application of which it has suspended, the reasons that gave rise to the suspension, and the date set for the termination of such suspension.

It will be noted that the European Convention refers to a time of war or other public emergency threatening the life of the nation. The ICCPR refers to a time of public emergency which threatens the life of the nation and the existence of which is officially proclaimed. The American Convention refers to a time of war, public danger, or other emergency that threatens the independence or security of a State Party. The list of rights expressly excluded from derogation is longer in the American Convention.

3.5 *1968 Resolution of the Inter-American Commission on Human Rights*

Already in 1968, the Inter-American Commission on Human Rights adopted and transmitted to Governments a ground-breaking *Resolution on the Protection of Human Rights in Connection with the Suspension of Constitutional Guarantees or the Stage of Siege.*[21] Because of the importance of this resolution we reproduce it fully below:

> *The Inter-American Commission on Human Rights*
> *Declares:*
> That the suspension of constitutional guarantees or 'state of siege' is compatible with the system of representative democratic government only if enacted under the following conditions:
> (a) When officially decreed under the procedure established in the respective constitutions,
> (b) When established in a measure strictly limited to the exigencies of the situation and with application limited to the duration thereof;
> (c) When adopted in case of war or other serious public emergency threatening the life of the nation or the security of the State;
> (d) When it does not entail any discrimination based on reasons of race, color, sex, language, religion, political or other opinions, national or social origin, economic status, birth or any other social conditions;
> (e) When it does not in any manner presuppose the suspension of the right to life, liberty or personal security, the right to protection against arbitrary detention, the right to due process of law, and the right to freedom of thought, conscience and religion;
> (f) When it does not in any manner presuppose restriction of the rule of law, or the provisions of the constitution, or alteration of the scope of the Powers of the State or of the proper exercise of the police powers.
> *States:*
> That the imposition of the state of siege or the suspension of instituted guarantees can be made the object, without prejudice to national sovereignty or the principle of non-intervention, of international

21 See *Inter-American Yearbook on Human Rights*, 1968. Washington D.C., 1973, p. 61.

control by means of the signing and ratification of a convention establishing the reciprocal undertaking.[22]

3.6 *General Comment No. 29 of the Human Rights Committee*

The International Covenant on Civil and Political Rights is the treaty that covers a far larger number of States Parties than any of the other two regional instruments and its General Comment No. 29, which elaborates on the meaning of Article 4 of the ICCPR, has attracted broad-based support among Governments and international human rights lawyers. General Comment 29, drawing upon the case law of the Human Rights Committee provides invaluable guidance on the substance of the law of derogations during emergencies. The Committee began by observing that Article 4 of the Covenant was of paramount importance for the system of protection for human rights under the Covenant.[23]

3.7 *Essential Requirements*

The Human Rights Committee underlined that measures derogating from the provisions of the Covenant must be of an exceptional temporary nature. Before a State moves to invoke Article 4, two fundamental conditions must be met: the situation must amount to a public emergency threatening the life of the nation, and the State party must have officially proclaimed a state of emergency. The latter requirement was essential for the maintenance of the principle of legality and rule of law at times when they were most needed. When proclaiming a state of emergency with consequences that could entail derogation from any provision of the Covenant, States must act within their constitutional and other provisions of law that govern such proclamation and the exercise of emergency powers.

3.8 *The Meaning of a Public Emergency*

Not every disturbance or catastrophe qualifies as a public emergency which threatens the life of the nation, as required by article 4, paragraph 1. The Covenant required that even during an armed conflict measures derogating from the Covenant were allowed only if and to the extent that the situation constituted a threat to the life of the nation. If States parties consider invoking article 4 in other situations than an armed conflict, they

22 This paragraph is explained by the fact that it was only a year later, in 1969, that the American Convention would be concluded.

23 General Comment No. 29 is reproduced in UN doc. HRI/Gen/1/Rev. 9, pp. 234–241.

should carefully consider the justification and why such a measure is necessary and legitimate in the circumstances.[24]

3.9 *Proportionality*

A fundamental requirement for any measure derogating from the Covenant is that such measures be limited to the extent strictly required by the exigencies of the situation. Derogation from some Covenant obligations in emergency situations is distinct from restrictions or limitations allowed even in normal times under several provisions of the Covenant. The obligation to limit any derogations to those strictly required by the exigencies of the situation reflected the principle of proportionality common to derogation and limitation powers. This condition requires that States parties provide careful justification not only for their decision to proclaim a state of emergency but also for any specific measures based on such a proclamation. The fact that some of the provisions of the Covenant have been listed in Article 4 (para.2), as not being subject to derogation does not mean that other articles in the Covenant may be subjected to derogations at will, even where a threat to the life of the nation exists.

3.10 *Peremptory Norms*

The Human Rights Committee considers that the enumeration of non-derogable provisions in Article 4 is related to, but not identical with, the question whether certain human rights obligations bear the nature of peremptory norms of international law. The Committee considers that the proclamation of certain provisions of the Covenant as being of a non-derogable nature in Article 4, paragraph 2, is to be seen partly as recognition of the peremptory nature of some fundamental rights ensured in treaty form in the Covenants (e.g., Articles 6 and 7). The category of peremptory norms extends beyond the list of non-derogable provisions as given in Article 4, paragraph 2. States parties may in no circumstances invoke Article 4 of the Covenant as justification for acting in violation of humanitarian law or peremptory norms of international law, for instance by taking hostages, by imposing collective punishments, through arbitrary deprivation of liberty or by deviating from fundamental principles of fair trial including the presumption of innocence.[25]

---

24 In the Lawless Case, the European Court of Human Rights defined a public emergency as "an exceptional situation of crisis or emergency which affects the whole population and constitutes a threat to the organized life of the community of which the State is composed." *Lawless v. Ireland*, Judgment of 7 April, 1961, para. 28.

25 *Ibid.*, para. 11.

3.11 *Crimes against Humanity*

In assessing the scope of legitimate derogation from the Covenant, one criterion can, in the view of the Human Rights Committee, be found in the definition of certain human rights violations as crimes against humanity. If action conducted under the authority of a State constitutes a basis for individual criminal responsibility for a crime against humanity by the persons involved in that action, Article 4 of the Covenant cannot be used as justification that a state of emergency exempted the State in question from its responsibility in relation to the same conduct. The recent codification of crimes against humanity, for jurisdictional purposes, in the Rome Statute of the International Criminal Court is of relevance to the interpretation of Article 4 of the Covenant.

3.12 *Notification*

The Human Rights Committee has emphasized that the notification by States parties should include full information about the measures taken and a clear explanation of the reasons for them, with full documentation attached regarding their law. Additional notifications are required if the State party subsequently taken further measures under Article 4, for instance by extending the duration of a state of emergency. The requirement of immediate notification applies equally in relation to the termination of derogation.

3.13 *The Prohibition of Torture*

By letter dated 11 October 2001, the then High Commissioner for Human Rights solicited the views of the Committee against Torture on how to ensure that the human rights covered by its mandate were maintained with a high visibility in the light of various State responses to the terrorist attacks in the United States of America on 11 September, 2001. In the spirit of that request the Committee against Torture decided to communicate directly with the States Parties of the Convention against Torture and Other Cruel, Inhuman or Degrading Treatment or Punishment[26] with the following statement:

> The Committee against Torture condemns utterly the terrorist attacks of September 11 and expresses its profound condolences to the victims, who were nationals of some 80 countries, including many State parties to the Convention against Torture and Other Cruel, Inhuman or Degrading Treatment or Punishment. The Committee is mindful of

26 New York, 1984. 1465 UNTS 85.

the terrible threat to international peace and security posed by these acts of international terrorism, as affirmed in Security Council resolution 1368. The Committee also notes that the Security Council in resolution 1373 identified the need to combat by all means, in accordance with the Charter of the United Nations, the threats caused by terrorist acts.

The Committee against Torture reminds States parties to the Convention of the non-derogable nature of most of the obligations undertaken by them in ratifying the Convention.

The obligations contained in Articles 2 (whereby "no exceptional circumstances whatsoever may be invoked as a justification of torture"), 15 (prohibiting confessions extorted by torture being admitted in evidence, except against the torturer), and 16 (prohibiting cruel, inhuman or degrading treatment or punishment) are three such provisions and must be observed in all circumstances.

The Committee against Torture is confident that whatever responses to the threat to international terrorism are adopted by States Parties, such responses will be in conformity with the obligations undertaken by them in ratifying the Convention against Torture.[27]

3.14 *Judicial Guarantees*

The Inter-American Court of Human Rights has on several occasions clarified the law governing states of siege or emergency in terms that are applicable internationally. In 1985, for example, the Court advised as follows, advice it has subsequently repeated on different occasions:

> In a democratic society, the rights and freedoms inherent in the human person, the guarantees applicable to them and the rule of law form a triad. Each component thereof defines itself, complements and depends on the others for its meaning...
>
> When guarantees are suspended, some legal restraints applicable to the acts of public authorities may differ from those in effect under normal conditions. These restraints may not be considered to be non-existent, however, nor can the government be deemed thereby to have acquired absolute powers that go beyond the circumstances justifying the grant of such exceptional legal measures. The Court has already noted, in this connection, that there exists an inseparable

27 CAT/C/XXVII/Misc.7, 22 November, 2001.

> bond between the principle of legality, democratic institutions and the rule of law.[28]

In an Advisory Opinion on Judicial Guarantees in States of Emergency (Art. 27(2), 25, and 8 American Convention on Human Rights)[29] the Inter-American Court affirmed the following:

- The general requirement that in any state of emergency there be appropriate means to control the measures taken, so that they are proportionate to the needs and do not exceed the strict limits imposed by the Convention or derived from it.
- States parties have an obligation to provide effective judicial remedies that must be substantiated in accordance with the rules of due process of law.
- The absence of an effective remedy to violations of the rights recognized by the Convention is itself a violation of the Convention by the State Party in which the remedy is lacking.
- The principles of due process of law cannot be suspended in states of exception insofar as they are necessary conditions for the procedural institutions regulated by the Convention to be considered judicial guarantees.
- The rule of law, representative democracy, and personal liberty are essential in the system for the protection of human rights contained in the American Convention.

3.15 *Margin of Appreciation*

In the case of *Ireland v. The United Kingdom* (1978), the European Court of Human Rights (ECtHR) declared:

> It falls in the first place to each Contracting State, with its responsibility for 'the life of the nation, to determine whether that life is threatened by a public emergency. ... By reason of their direct and continuous contact with the pressing needs of the moment, the national authorities are in principle in a better position than the international judge, to decide ... on the presence of such an emergency. ... In this matter, article 15(1) leaves those authorities a wide margin of appreciation.[30]

---

28 Advisory Opinion OC-5785 of November 13, 1985, Series A. No. 5, para. 66.
29 Advisory Opinion OC-9/87 of October 6, 1987, Series A No. 9.
30 *Ireland v. The United Kingdom*, 18 January 1978, Series A, No.25; (1979–80) 2

4 The Concept of Protection

The notion of protection (initially domestic protection) may be traced back to very early times as organized human societies were emerging and notions of law and justice were evolving. In his study, *Freedom in the Ancient World*, H.J. Muller showed how law codes, written or unwritten, provided protection to the individual and he traced 'the efforts of kings to protect ordinary men against the abuses of power and privilege'.[31] Emmanuel Bello found notions akin to protection in African customary humanitarian law and reported that, while not generally the case, during armed conflicts in certain parts of Africa some tribes 'took pride in according respect and human rights to women, children and old persons'.[32] In Asia, Alexandrowicz found that there existed, historically high standards of protection of foreigners irrespective of religion or civilization.[33]

In Europe, the sixteenth century saw the development of the institution of 'Protecting Powers' as European powers obtained, through capitulation treaties, the right to exercise exclusive, extra-territorial jurisdiction over their nationals in the Ottoman Empire, and later on in the other independent countries of the Middle and Far East. The institution of protecting powers, which could also be found in diplomatic and consular practice evolved subsequently and grew into the 'cornerstone of the system of implementation of the Geneva conventions' of 1949 on the laws of armed conflicts.[34]

The use of treaties providing for the protection of human rights, which was known even in the practice of the ancient Greeks, began to assume prominence in the seventeenth century. The Treaty of Westphalia (1648) sought to ensure equality of rights for Roman Catholics and Protestants in Germany. During the seventeenth century, some governments undertook in peace treaties to respect the rights of Roman Catholic subjects of Protestant princes. In 1774 Turkey undertook vis-à-vis Russia to protect the Christian religion and its churches within its territory. The Congress of Vienna of 1815 provided for the free exercise of religion and for equality,

---

EHRR 25, para. 207. See, similarly, *Aksoy v. Turkey* (App. 1987/93), Judgment of 18 December 1996; 23 *EHRR*, para. 68 of the judgment.

31 H.J. Muller, *Freedom in the Ancient World* (London: Secker and Warburg, 1962), 58–59. See also, J. Shotwell, *The Long Way to Freedom* (New York: Columbia University Press, 1960).

32 E. Bello, *African Customary Humanitarian law* (1980), 29.

33 C.H. Alexandrowicz, "The Afro-Asian World and the Law of Nations (Historical Aspects)," 123, *RCADI* (1968), I, 117–214, at 151.

34 For a concise and useful history of the institution of Protecting Power, see G. Abi-Saab, "The Implementation of Humanitarian Law" in A. Cassese (Ed.), *The New Humanitarian Law of Armed Conflict* (The Hague: Martinus Nijhoff, 1979), 310–348 at 311–318.

irrespective of religion, in various cantons of Switzerland as well as for the equality of Christian denominations in Germany. The Congress also contained provisions aiming at the improvement of the civil status of Jews.[35]

The doctrine and practice of 'humanitarian intervention' may also be included among the antecedents of the concept of 'international protection.' In previous centuries, when the treatment by a state of its own population was so abusive and cruel that it shocked the conscience of humanity, other states claimed the right to threaten or use force in order to assist the oppressed persons. Setting aside the issue of the validity of such interventions in contemporary international law, the practice does at least offer guidance with regard to one set of circumstances when international protection would be warranted: when atrocities reach such a scale as to shock the conscience of humanity.

The concept of international protection may, furthermore, be traced in the movements for the abolition of slavery, for the establishment of international humanitarian law concerning the conduct of hostilities and the protection of human rights during periods of armed conflict and for the development of international social and labour legislation which the ILO has pioneered since its establishment.

The institution of diplomatic protection, one of the hallowed institutions of international law, has also contributed to the development of the concept of international protection of human rights. Diplomatic protection proceeds from a state's right to protect its nationals abroad. As the Permanent Court of International Justice stated in the Mavrommatis Palestine Concession Case: "It is an elementary principle of international law that a state is entitled to protect its subjects, when injured by acts contrary to international law committed by another state, from whom they have been unable to obtain satisfaction through the ordinary channels."[36] In traditional international law, the responsibility of states for damage done in their territory to the person or property of foreigners rested on the international standard of justice, and the principle of the equality of nationals and aliens. As the General Claims Commission held in the Neer Case, the propriety of governmental acts should be put to the test of international standards.

In an important submission, F.V. Garcia-Amador, former rapporteur of the International Law Commission, argued that what was formerly the object of these two principles – the protection of the person and of his prop-

35 See E. Schwelb, "Human Rights," in *Encyclopedia Britannica*, Vol. 8, 1974, 1183–1189.

36 Mavrommatis Pelestine Concessions Case, PCIJ, ser A. No.2 (1924), 12.

erty – is now intended to be accomplished by the international recognition of the essential rights of human beings.[37]

In some of the peace treaties, in special minorities treaties and in declarations made after World War I, some states of central and eastern Europe and a state in the Middle East (Iraq) accepted obligations towards their racial, linguistic and religious minorities to the effect that all of their nationals were to be equal before the law and were to enjoy the same civil and political rights without distinction as to race, language or religion. The relevant treaties provided that their provisions constituted obligations of international concern rather than domestic matters and all were placed under the guarantee of the League of Nations.

At the drafting of the United Nations Charter in San Francisco, the question arose expressly whether the Charter should define the role of the United Nations in terms of 'promotion' or 'protection'. The drafters opted for language calling for the achievement of international cooperation in promoting and encouraging respect for human rights and for fundamental freedoms. Notwithstanding the use of the term 'promotion', the practice of the United Nations has confirmed the competence of the Organization to act for the protection of human rights. As an authoritative commentator wrote in 1972:

> In the actual practice of the various organs of the United Nations over the past 25 years the obstacles to taking action based on the human rights provisions of the Charter have proved to be far less formidable than the cleavage of theoretical opinions of scholars and of abstract statements by governments would lead one to assume. In the practice of the United Nations and its Members neither the vagueness and generality of the human rights clauses of the Charter nor the domestic jurisdiction clause have prevented the United Nations from considering, investigating, and judging concrete human rights situations, provided there was a majority strong enough and wishing strongly enough to attempt to influence the particular development...[38]

An expert on the International Committee of the Red Cross (ICRC), discussing the protection functions of the ICRC, placed them into two categories: direct protection and indirect protection. He submitted that each of the

---

37 F.V. Garcia-Amador, "Report on State Responsibility," *YBILC*, 1956, Vol.II, 173–231, at 203.

38 E. Schwelb, "The International Court of Justice and the Human Rights Clauses of the Charter," 66 *AJIL* (1972), 337–351, at 341.

following three basic roles of the ICRC had a direct and an indirect dimension: (1) *ad hoc* diplomacy; (2) development of law; and (3) application of the law.[39] There is much merit in this frame of direct and indirect protection, which we believe offers a conceptual approach corresponding mostly closely to international protection as practiced in the United Nations.

4.1 *The Responsibility to Protect*

The report of the International Commission on Intervention and state Sovereignty launched the concept of the responsibility to protect.[40] In the Commission's view, the responsibility to protect embraced three specific responsibilities: the responsibility to prevent, namely, to address both the root causes and direct causes of internal conflict and other man-made crises putting populations at risk; the responsibility to react, namely, to respond to situations of compelling human need with appropriate measures, which may include coercive measures like sanctions and international prosecution, and in extreme cases military intervention; the responsibility to rebuild, namely, to provide, particularly after a military intervention, full assistance with recovery, reconstruction and reconciliation, addressing the causes of the harm the intervention was designed to halt or avert.

The Commission was firm in its view that prevention was the single most important dimension of the responsibility to protect. Prevention options should always be exhausted before intervention was contemplated, and more commitment and resources must be devoted to it. The exercise of the responsibility to prevent and react should always involve less intrusive and coercive measures before more coercive and intrusive ones are applied.

The United Nations Summit of world leaders, meeting to mark the organizations 60th anniversary in 2005 endorsed the responsibility to protect and declared their readiness, if need be, to refer to the UN Security Council (UNSC) for its attention situations of genocide, crimes against humanity and war crimes.

4.1 *Preventive, Curative and Remedial or Compensatory Protection*

International protection may be grouped into three categories: anticipatory or preventive, mitigatory or curative, remedial or compensatory. *Preventive protection* means that the national authorities, regional organiza-

39 D.P. Forsythe, *Humanitarian Politics: The International Committee of the Red Cross* (Baltimore: The Johns Hopkins University Press, 1977), 28–32.

40 International Commission on Intervention and State Sovereignty, *The Responsibility to Protect*, December 2001. See also *The Responsibility to Protect: Research, Bibliography, Background*, December 2001.

tions, or the United Nations, should try to anticipate and head off potential situations of gross violations of human rights before they occur. This is a newer thrust in the efforts of the human rights movement and prevention is still in its infancy.[41] Prevention should be an essential part of any national protection system.

Among the preventive measures taken by international bodies, mention may be made of urgent appeals addressed on behalf of victims or of interim measures undertaken on their behalf. On some occasions the UNSC has met to consider a situation and to bring its influence to bear on those involved. Special Procedures of the UN Human Rights Council address urgent appeals to Governments in cases of concern. The UN High Commissioner for Human Rights may do likewise or may make public statements expressing concern. The Secretary-General may intercede if he considers that this could be helpful. In the European Commission and the Inter-American Commission on Human Rights, the secretaries of these organs have an established practice of interceding urgently with a government if, from the facts reported to them, they conclude that an individual is in serious danger of having irreparable harm done to them. The good offices of international officials such as the UN High Commissioner for Human Rights, the Director-General of the ILO may be called upon.[42]

Aside from these limited measures, such as appeals, interim measures, or the use of humanitarian good offices, the area of anticipation and prevention represents one of the major gaps in the arrangements for the international protection of human rights. Let us cite, in this regard, the following statement which was made by Dr. Theo C. van Boven, the then Director of the United Nations Division of Human Rights to the then Commission on Human Rights, in 1980:

> We are frequently faced in the United Nations with serious and urgent problems of violations of human rights which arise in different parts of the world, but, apart from statements of the Secretary-General issued in a humanitarian spirit, or the exercise of his good offices in certain cases, the organization is mostly unable to take action in a situation where every day counts heavily notwithstanding the hope and expectations of the international community for such action. In the ILO, for example, the Director-General has been granted the compe-

---

41 See, L-A Sicilianos, *et al.* (Eds.), *The Prevention of Human Rights Violations* (The Hague, New York: Martinus Nijhoff Publishers, 2001).

42 See B.G. Ramcharan, *Humanitarian Good Offices in International Law* (The Hague: Martinus Nijhoff, 1983).

> tence, in urgent cases, to approach the government concerned to receive a mission from the organization urgently to look into allegations of violations of trade unions rights within the country in question. ... We, in the United Nations, similarly receive many complaints and disturbing reports about grave human rights problems in this as well as in other countries... but there is no similar possibility for action open to us. In my view, this is a major deficiency in the arrangements.[43]

The situation has not changed much since then.

Curative protection involves efforts to mitigate and stop gross violations of human rights that may be taking place. The UNSC, the UN Human Rights Council (HRC), Special Procedures of the HRC, the United Nations High Commissioner for Human Rights, and the United Nations Secretary-General endeavours to engage in mitigatory and curative protection.

Various procedures exist within different international organizations, whose aims may be said to stop or to mitigate excesses being committed, or to cure or redress situations giving rise to such excesses. Among these may be mentioned: the United Nations procedures for dealing with complaints of violations of human rights; ILO's complaints procedures; UNESCO's complaints procedures; Inter-governmental complaints procedures, such as those under the European Convention on Human Rights, the American Convention on Human Rights or the International Covenant on Civil and Political Rights; investigation and fact-finding under various procedures in the United Nations, ILO, the Council of Europe and the OAS, visits on-the spot or the establishment of international presences; the activities of the ICRC, and the United Nations High Commissioner for Human Rights, The UNHCR; the activities of non-governmental organizations; the exercise of good offices; and public denunciations of violations of human rights.

Some of the procedures within the different international organizations may be said to have the objective of providing protection through remedies or compensation. Of particular significance in this regard are the petition systems under the European, African, and American Conventions on Human Rights and under the Optional Protocol to the International Covenant on Civil and Political Rights. Judicial measures of protection such as those provided by the European Court of Human Rights, the African Court of Human Rights, and the Inter-American Court of Human Rights are also relevant in this regard. Also related are the efforts currently being made within the United Nations to provide reconstruction assistance to countries which have experienced extensive violations of human rights, as well

43 T.C. van Boven, *People Matter* (Amsterdam, Meulenhoff, 1982), 73.

as to individuals who have been subjected to such violations.[44]

Remedial and compensatory protection involves processes of establishing the truth about what took place in a situation of gross violations of human rights, bringing perpetrators to justice where possible, and providing redress to victims of gross violations of human rights or to their families. Truth and reconciliation commissions are bodies that seek to ascertain and record what took place. National or hybrid courts may deal with justice issues. So might the ICC or ad hoc tribunals such as the International Criminal Tribunals for the Former Yugoslavia and Rwanda, the Sierra Leone Court and the Cambodia Court.

It should be pointed out that although we have referred to some procedures under the headings of preventive/anticipatory; curative/mitigatory and remedial/compensatory, many procedures in fact perform functions belonging to more than one of these categories.

4.2 *The Duty to Ensure*

In the Velásquez Rodriguez Case (1988), the Inter-American Court of Human Rights[45] dealt with Article 1(1) of the American Convention on Human Rights which provides as follows: "1. The States Parties to this Convention undertake to respect the rights and freedoms recognized herein and to ensure to all persons subject to their jurisdiction the free and full exercise of those rights and freedoms, without any discrimination ..." The Court commented that in effect, this article charges the State Parties with the fundamental duty to respect and guarantee the rights recognized in the Convention. Any impairment of those rights which can be attributed under the rules of international law to the action or omission of any public authority constitutes an act imputable to the State, which assumes responsibility in the terms provided by the Convention.

The Court went on to clarify the meaning of the obligation 'to ensure'. The obligation of the State Party, it held, is to ensure the free and full exercise of the rights recognized by the Convention to every person subject to its jurisdiction. This obligation implies the duty of the States Parties to organize the governmental apparatus and, in general, all the structures through which public power is exercised, so that they are capable of juridically ensuring the free and full enjoyment of human rights. As a consequence of this obligation, the States must prevent, investigate and punish any violation of the rights recognized by the Convention and, moreover, if

44 A United Nations Fund for Victims of Torture has been in existence since 1991.

45 4 Inter-Am. Ct. H.R. (ser C).

possible attempt to restore the right violated and provide compensation as warranted for damages resulting from the violation.

The State is obligated, the Court continued, to investigate every situation involving a violation of the rights protected by the Convention. If the State apparatus acted in such a way that the violation went unpunished and the victim's full enjoyment of such rights was not restored as soon as possible, the State had a failed to comply with its duty to ensure the free and full exercise of those rights to the persons within its jurisdiction. The same was true when the State allowed private persons or groups to act freely and with impunity to the detriment of the rights recognized in the Convention.

In certain circumstances, the Court recognized, it might be difficult to investigate acts that violated an individual's rights. The duty to investigate, like the duty to prevent, was not breached merely because the investigation did not produce a satisfactory result. Nevertheless, it must be undertaken in a serious manner and not as a mere formality preordained to be ineffective. An investigation must have an objective and be assumed by the State as its own legal duty, not as a step taken by private interests that depended upon the initiative of the victim or his family or upon their offer of proof, without an effective search for the truth by the government. This was true regardless of what agent was eventually found responsible for the violation. Where the acts of private parties that violated the Convention were not seriously investigated, those parties were aided in a sense by the government, thereby making the State responsible on the international plain.

In the case of a disappeared person, for example, the duty to investigate the facts continued as long as there was uncertainty about the fate of the person who had disappeared.

4.3 *The Duty to Respect, Ensure, Fulfil, Protect*

In General Comment No. 16, which dealt with the equal right of men and women to the enjoyment of all economic, social and cultural rights, the Committee on Economic, Social and Cultural Rights affirmed that the enjoyment of human rights on the basis of equality between men and women must be understood comprehensively. Guarantees of non-discrimination and equality in international human rights treaties mandated both de facto and de jure equality. De jure (or formal) equality and de facto (or substantive) equality are different but interconnected concepts. Formal equality is achieved if a law or policy treats men and women in a neutral manner. Substantive equality is concerned, in addition, with the effects of laws, policies and practices and with ensuring that they do not maintain, but rather alleviate, the inherent disadvantage that particular groups experience.[46]

The principle of non-discrimination, the Committee continued, is the corollary of the principle of equality. It prohibits differential treatment of a person or group of persons based on his/her particular status or situation, such as race, colour, sex, language, religion, political and other opinion, national or social origin, property, birth, or other status, such as age, ethnicity, disability, marital, refugee or migrant status. Discrimination against women was 'any distinction, exclusion, or restriction made on the basis of sex which has the effect or purpose of impairing or nullifying the recognition, enjoyment or exercise by women, irrespective of their marital status, on a basis of equality of men and women, of human rights and fundamental freedoms in the political, economic,. Social, cultural, civil or any other field', as defined in Article 1 of the Convention on the Elimination of All Forms of Discrimination against Women.[47]

The Committee discussed the obligation to respect as follows:

> The obligation to respect requires States parties to refrain from discriminatory actions that directly or indirectly result in the denial of the equal right of men and women to their enjoyment of economic, social and cultural rights. Respecting the right obliges States parties not to adopt, and to repeal laws and rescind policies, administrative measures and programmes that do not conform with the right protected by Article 3. In particular, it is incumbent upon States parties to take into account the effect of apparently gender neutral laws, policies and programmes and to consider whether they could result in a negative impact on the ability of men and women to enjoy their human rights on a basis of equality.[48]

Turning to the obligation to protect, the Committee stated the following:

> The obligation to protect requires States parties to take steps aimed directly at the elimination of prejudices, customary and all other practices that perpetuate the notion of inferiority or superiority of either of the sexes, and stereotyped roles for men and women. States parties' obligation to protect under article 3 of ICESCR[49] includes,

46 HRI/GEN/Rev.9, pp. 114–115.
47 *Ibid.*, p. 115. New York, 1979. 1249 UNTS 13.
48 *Ibid.*, p. 117.
49 International Covenant of Economic, Social and Cultural Rights (ICESCR). New York, 1966. 993 UNTS 3.

> *inter alia* the respect and adoption of constitutional and legislative provisions on the equal right of men and women to enjoy all human rights and the prohibition of discrimination of any kind; the adoption of legislation to eliminate discrimination and to prevent third parties from interfering directly or indirectly with the enjoyment of this right; the adoption of administrative measures and programmes, as well as the establishment of public institutions, agencies and programmes to protect women against discrimination.
>
> States parties have an obligation to monitor and regulate the conduct of non-State actors to ensure that they do not violate the equal right of men and women to enjoy economic, social and cultural rights. This obligation applies, for example, in cases where public services have been partially or fully privatized.[50]

As regards the obligation to fulfil, the Committee commented:

> The obligation to fulfil requires States parties to take steps to ensure that in practice, men and women enjoy their economic, social and cultural rights on a basis of equality. Such steps should include:
>
> - To make available and accessible appropriate remedies, such as compensation, reparation, restitution, rehabilitation, guarantees of non-repetition, declaration, declarations, public apologies, educational programmes and prevention programmes.
> - To establish appropriate venues for redress such as courts and tribunals or administrative mechanisms that are accessible to all on the basis of equality, including the poorest and most disadvantaged and marginalized men and women.
> - To develop monitoring mechanisms to ensure that the implementation of laws and policies aimed at promoting the equal enjoyment of economic, social and cultural rights by men and women do not have unintended adverse effects on disadvantaged or marginalized individuals or groups, particularly women and girls.
> - To design and implement policies and programmes to give long-term effect to the economic, social and cultural rights of both men and women on the basis of equality. These may include the adoption of temporary special measures to accelerate women's equal enjoyment of their rights, gender audits, and gender-specific allocation of resources.
> - To conduct human rights education and training programmes

50 *Ibid.*, p. 117.

for judges and public officials.

- To conduct awareness-raising and training programmes on equality for workers involved in the realization of economic, social and cultural rights at the grass-roots level.
- To integrate, in formal and non-formal education, the principle of the equal rights of men and women to the enjoyment of economic, social and cultural rights, and to promote equal participation of men and women, boys and girls, in schools and other education programmes.
- To promote equal representation of men and women in public office and decision-making bodies.
- To promote equal participation of men and women in development planning, decision-making and in the benefits of development and all programmes related to the realization of economic, social and cultural rights.[51]

4.4 *Violations of the Obligations to Respect, Ensure, Protect, Fulfil*

In a series of general comments, the Committee on Economic, Social and Cultural Rights has expounded on the duty to respect, protect and to fulfil particular rights in the ICESCR and on violations of these obligations. In General Comment No. 14, for example, dealing with the right to the highest attainable standard of health, the Committee reaffirmed what it had stated in General Comment No. 3 that States parties had a core obligation to ensure the satisfaction of, at the very least, minimum essential levels of each of the rights contained in the Covenant, including essential primary health care. The Committee proceeded to deal with violations of the obligations to respect, to protect and to fulfil in the following terms:

4.5 *Violations of the Obligation to Respect*

Violations of the obligation to respect are those State actions, policies or laws that contravene the standards set out in Article 12 of the ICESCR and are likely to result in bodily harm, unnecessary morbidity and preventable mortality.

4.6 *Violations of the Obligation to Protect*

Violations of the obligation to protect follow from the failure to take all necessary measures to safeguard persons within their jurisdiction from infringements of the right to health by third parties.

---

51 *Ibid.*, pp. 117–118.

4.8 *Violations of the Obligation to Fulfil*

Violations of the obligation to fulfil occur through the failure of States parties to take all necessary steps to ensure the realization of the right to health.[52]

5 Conclusion

As will have been seen in the foregoing chapter, there is considerable guidance to be found in international law when it comes to the concepts of prevention, protection, respect, ensure, and fulfil. The future mission international human rights law and of universally-binding human rights norms is to work for their faithful implementation in practice, in all countries.

52 HRI/GEN/1Rev.9, pp 90 – 91. See similarly, p. 105 ff. on violations of the right to water; pp. 116–117 and 121–122 violations of Article 3 on equal rights between men and women; pp. 133–134 on violations of Article 15; pp. 147–148, violations of the right to work.

9 Human Dignity, Equality, Justice and Survival Rights

1 Introduction

Respect for, and protection of, human dignity is an animating and guiding principle of the whole human rights project announced by the UN Charter and the Universal Declaration of Human Rights.[1] Its inspirational force guided the drafting of the Universal Declaration and, subsequently, the international and regional human rights treaties inspired by the Declaration. In order to understand its legal content one needs to consider its philosophical origins, to trace its application in the development of human rights norms, its application in the domains of survival and livelihood rights, peace, development, human rights and humanitarianism, and to see how the concept has been applied by international, regional and national courts. We discuss some of these issues in the chapter that follows.

2 Human Dignity

The concept of dignity signifies worth or estimation. In modern moral philosophy, especially that of Kant, dignity is considered as a universal attribute, an offshoot of the capacity for self-consciousness and practical reason.

The entrenchment of human dignity as a universal human rights norm was one of the great normative innovations of the 1940s. The UN Charter makes several references to the principles of the dignity and equality of all human beings. In the Preamble of the Charter, the Peoples of the United Nations reaffirmed their faith in fundamental rights, in the dignity and worth of the human person and in the equal rights of men and women.

During the drafting of the Universal Declaration of Human Rights, dignity as a right had been challenged by the representative of South Africa. Mrs. Eleanor Roosevelt, representative of the USA and Chairperson of the UN Commission on Human Rights, recalled that dignity had been considered carefully by the Human Rights Commission, which had included it in order to emphasize that every human being is worthy of respect.[2] The Commission had decided to include it in order to emphasize the inherent dignity of all mankind.[3]

Human dignity in international law was the focus of a book by Ginev-

---

1 Paris, 10 December 1948, GA res. 217 A.

2 Glendon, *op. cit.*, p. 146.

3 A/C.3/SR 98, reproduced in Schabas, *op. cit.*, p. 2169.

ra Le Moli, published in 2021.[4] Le Moli discusses two competing conceptions of dignity, sovereign dignity and human dignity. The first related to the dignity of sovereigns, or heads of state. The second related to the dignity of human beings which, in her view eventually overtook and largely supplanted sovereign dignity.[5] On the intellectual origins of the concept of human dignity, Le Moli places emphasis on Christian and Kantian conceptions "due to their distinctive historical influence on the shaping of international law."[6]

This may be a culturally influenced understanding, not taking account of concepts akin to human dignity found in non-Western philosophical systems. Writing about democracy in Ancient India, J. Nehru, first Prime Minister of India, suggested that the democratic way was well known and a common method of functioning in social life, in local government, trade guilds, religious assemblies and similar gatherings. He quoted the Marquis of Zetland as follows:

> ... [I]t may come as a surprise to many to learn that in the assemblies of the Buddhists in India two thousand years ago are to be found the rudiments of our own parliamentary practice of the present day. The dignity of the Assembly was preserved by the appointment of a special officer – the embryo of 'Mr Speaker' in the House of Commons. A second officer was appointed whose duty it was to see that when necessary a quorum was secured – the prototype of the Parliamentary Chief Whip in our own system. A member initiating business did so in the form of a motion which was then open to discussion. In some cases this was done once only, in others three times, thus anticipating the practice of Parliament in requiring that a Bill be read a third time before it becomes law. If discussion disclosed a difference of opinion the matter was decided by the vote of the majority, the voting being by ballot.[7]

In an analysis of Mahatma Gandhi's concept of freedom, Dennis Dalton[8]

4 Ginevra Le Moli, *Human Dignity in International Law* (Cambridge, Cambridge University Press, 2021).

5 *Ibid.*, p. 4.

6 *Ibid.*, p. 8.

7 J. Nehru, *The Discovery of India,* pp. 297–298, reproduced in K.T. Narasimha Char, *The Quintessence of Nehru* (London, Allen and Unwin, 1961), p. 43.

8 Dennis Dalton, *Gandhi* (New York, Columbia University Press, 1993, 2000). Dennis Dalton was Professor of Political Science at Columbia University. Earlier in his career he had taught in Nepal and India.

found that Gandhi considered that one is liberated as one gains greater self-knowledge and consequent self-mastery. Liberation evolves from a higher consciousness, an awareness of the unity of all being, the identify of oneself with the universal Self or Atman.[9]

Gandhi clearly distinguished between liberty and license. For him, "... the proper question is not what the rights of a citizen are, but rather what constitutes the duties of a citizen. Fundamental rights can only be those rights the exercise of which is not only in the interest of the citizen but that of the whole world.... The beauty of it is that the very performance of a duty secures us our right. Rights cannot be divorced from duties. This is how satyagraha was born, for I was always striving to decide what my duty was."[10]

According to Le Moli, human dignity first entered the field of international law as a religious concept in the second half of the nineteenth century and then underwent a transformation into a secularized concept, as a condition for its generalization after the Second World War. [11] She thinks that "human dignity came to nuance, then influence and, ultimately, fundamentally transform the very architecture of international law".[12]

Le Moli suggests that there are two broad strands in the conceptualization of human dignity: (i) a religious perspective, which looks at the concept as connected to the divine or to a metaphysical account; and (ii) what could be called a set of secular accounts that have enabled the development of human rights.[13] She however recognizes the contemporary invocation of the concept of human dignity that started with the drafting of the International Bill of Rights. She assesses the two Covenants on human rights introduced a legal novelty into the international human rights project started in 1945. They declared in the second paragraph of the Preamble: "Recognizing that these rights derive from the inherent dignity of the human person."[14]

Le Moli identifies what she considers two strands of uses of the principle of human dignity: the first identifies human dignity with the whole of morality. According to which acting against morality is, as such, acting against human dignity or, more precisely, against the agent's own human dignity. Second, the principle of human dignity operates also at the level of interpretation of international principles and norms, serving an auxiliary

---

9 *Ibid.*, p. 2.
10 *Ibid.*, p. xii.
11 *Ibid.*, p. 6.
12 Le Moli, *op. cit.*, p. 4.
13 *Ibid.*, p. 319.
14 *Ibid.*, p. 150.

function. The principle of human dignity, she adds, serves as a general interpretative guideline, in the sense that whenever there are unclear norms or doubts about their interpretation, it demands to consider requirements of humanity in interpreting international rules, reorganizing the order of priorities.[15]

Human dignity defines not only the core international crimes but also the nature of the prosecutorial system. Crimes that are contrary to the protection of human dignity deserve to have a prosecution that supersedes national courts and can provide an international justice for horrors committed by *hostes humani generis* that share the conscience of humankind, beyond concerns of State sovereignty.[16]

Le Moli suggests that human dignity was adopted as a general principle of law underpinning *jus cogens* provisions and source of legal effects of peremptory norms.[17] And she sees the foundation of a possible fourth constitutive stage of human dignity. In this stage, dignity expands once again its universal scope beyond the individual and collective human nature and, thus, beyond the human circle. "It once again silences its exclusionary character" and now covers "[the dignity of nature".[18]

The UN's Agenda 2030 sets out in Sustainable Development Goal 16 the objective of achieving by 2030 a world of peace, justice, inclusive, effective and strong institutions. What is aimed for here is absolutely vital to the future of humankind: universal respect for human rights, democratic governance, the prevention of conflicts, fairness in societies, nationally and internationally, and governance that is grounded in democracy, respect for human rights, and upholding of the Purposes and Principles of the UN Charter as well as of the Universal Declaration of Human Rights.

The path to the adoption of SDG 16 was not a straightforward one, and efforts for its implementation to date have not been straightforward either. There were skirmishes before its adoption. There were those who pushed for a more explicit affirmation of human rights as central to the implementation of the SDGs and those who resisted this. The result was a compromise framed in terms of peace, justice, and effective institutions. These are nevertheless powerful concepts that if pursued meaningfully and in good faith could have a solid impact on the future of the world. On the other

15 *Ibid.*, p. 184. See also, p. 187: human dignity as a right; p. 216, human dignity as human rights law; and p. 239: the right to dignity.

16 *Ibid.*, p. 300.

17 *Ibid.*, p. 304. She comments: "Human dignity and humanitas shape not only the definition of core international crimes but also the nature and actual operativity of their prosecutorial systems", p. 367.

18 *Ibid.*, pp. 323 and 327.

hand, if mere lip-service is paid to them the results will be hollow.

Some Governments and NGOs have partnered to support the implementation of SDG 16 and there have been useful outputs from research institutions. On peace, there have been NGO reports indicating a high number of countries experiencing or at risk of conflict. On justice, there have been reports analyzing how the pursuit of justice could help shore up peace. On the need for effective institutions, there have been studies on the meaning of representativity and the meaning of inclusiveness.

3 Equality

Equality is a foundation normative principle in every human rights instrument, international or regional. In this section we look at the elucidation of this great principle in the jurisprudence and practice of the leading supervisory bodies, beginning with the Human Rights Committee.

3.1 *General Comment 18/37 of the Human Rights Committee (Equality and Non-Discrimination)*

In General Comment 18/37 of 9 November 1989, the Human Rights Committee provided useful guidance on the provisions of the International Covenant on Civil and Political Rights dealing with equality and non-discrimination. The Committee noted that the Covenant neither defined the term 'discrimination' nor indicated what constituted discrimination. It noted, however, that article 1 of the International Convention on the Elimination of All Forms of Racial Discrimination[19] provided that the term 'racial discrimination' shall mean any distinction, exclusion, restriction or preference based on race, colour, descent or national or ethnic origin which has the purpose or effect of nullifying or impairing the recognition, enjoyment or exercise, on an equal footing, of human rights and fundamental freedoms in the political, economic, social, cultural or any other field of public life. Similarly, Article 1 of the Convention on the Elimination of All Forms of Discrimination against Women provides that 'discrimination against women' shall mean any distinction, exclusion or restriction made on the basis of sex which has the effect or purpose of impairing or nullifying the recognition, enjoyment or exercise by women, irrespective of their marital status, on a basis of equality of men and women, of human rights and fundamental freedoms in the political, economic, social, cultural, civil or any other field.

While the conventions referred to dealt only with cases of discrimination on specific grounds, the Human Rights Committee believed that the

19 New York, 1966. 660 UNTS 195.

term 'discrimination' as used in the ICCPR should be understood to imply any distinction, exclusion, restriction or preference which is based on any ground such as race, colour, sex, language, religion, political or other opinion, national or social origin, property, birth or other status, and which has the purpose or effect of nullifying or impairing the recognition, enjoyment or exercise by all persons, on an equal footing, of all rights and freedoms. However, the enjoyment of rights and freedoms on an equal footing does not mean identical treatment in every instance. The Committee also pointed out that the principle of equality sometimes requires States Parties to take affirmative action in order to diminish or eliminate conditions which cause or help to perpetuate discrimination prohibited by the Covenant.

In an important clarification, the Human Rights Committee expressed the view that Article 26 of the ICCPR does not merely duplicate the guarantee already provided in Article 2 but provides in itself an autonomous right. It prohibits discrimination in law or in fact in any field regulated and protected by public authorities. Article 26 is therefore concerned with the obligations imposed on States Parties in regard to their legislation and the application thereof. Thus, when legislation is adopted by a State Party, it must comply with the requirement of Article 26 that its content should not be discriminatory. In other words, the application of the principle of non-discrimination contained in Article 26 is not limited to those rights which are provided for in the ICCPR.[20]

---

20 In the case of S.W.M. Broeks (Communication No. 172/1984, the Human Rights Committee considered the provisions of Articles 84 and 85 of the Netherlands Civil Code which imposed equal rights and obligations on spouses with regard to their joint income. However, under section 13, subsection 1(1) of the Unemployment Benefits Act (WWV), a married woman, in order to receive WWV benefits, had to prove that she was a 'breadwinner' – a condition that did not apply to married men. The Human Rights Committee held that this was a differentiation which appeared on one level to be one of status but was in fact one of sex, placing married women at a disadvantage compared with married men. Such a differentiation, in the Committee's view, was not reasonable. The circumstances in which Mrs Broeks found herself at the material time and the application of the then valid Netherlands law made her a victim of a violation, based on sex, of Article 26 of the International Covenant on Civil and Political Rights, because she was denied a social security benefit on an equal footing with men. The Committee was of the view that the State party should offer Mrs Broeks an appropriate remedy (The Netherlands had changed the law by then). See International Covenant on Civil and Political Rights. Selected Decisions of the Human Rights Committee under the Optional Protocol. Vol. 2. Seventeenth to thirty-second sessions (October 1982 – April 1988. UN publication, Sales No. E.89.XI1, pp. 196–201. See similarly the case of F.H. Zwaan-de Fries, *Ibid.*, pp. 209–214.

Finally, the Human Rights Committee observed that not every differentiation of treatment will constitute discrimination, if the criteria for such differentiation are reasonable and objective and if the aim is to achieve a purpose which is legitimate under the ICCPR.[21]

3.2 *General Comment 4/13 of the Human Rights Committee (Gender Equality)*

The Human Rights Committee, in General Comment 4/13, of 28 July 1991, provided important guidance on the international law of human rights regarding gender equality, and specifically under Article 2(1), 3, and 26 of the International Covenant on Civil and Political Rights. Importantly, the Committee began with the observation that these articles require not only measures of protection but also affirmative action designed to ensure the positive enjoyment of rights. This cannot be done simply by enacting laws. Hence more information has generally been required regarding the role of women in practice with a view to ascertaining what measures in addition to purely legislative measures of protection have been or are being taken to give effect to the precise and positive obligations under Article 3 and to ascertain what progress is being made or what factors or difficulties are being met in this regard. However, the positive obligation undertaken by States Parties may itself have an inevitable impact on legislation or administrative measures specifically designed to regulate matters other than those dealt with in the ICCPR but which may adversely affect rights recognized in the ICCPR. It mentioned as an example the degree to which immigration laws which distinguish between a male and a female citizen may or may not adversely affect the scope of the right of the women to marriage to non-citizens or to hold public office.

The Human Rights Committee advised that it might assist States Parties if special attention were given to a review by specially appointed bodies or institutions of laws or measures which inherently draw a distinction between men and women in so far as those laws or measures adversely affect the rights provided for in the ICCPR. The Committee also considered that it might help the States Parties in implementing this obligation if more use could be made of existing means of international cooperation with a view to exchanging experience and organizing assistance in solving the practical problems connected with ensuring of equal rights for men and women.[22]

---

21 See M. Nowak, *U.N. Convention on Civil on Political Rights. CCPR Commentary* (Kehl, Germany: N.P. Engel Publisher, 2005), 1109–1111.

22 *U.N. Convention on Civil on Political Rights. CCPR Commentary*, 1091.

4 Justice

The philosopher Mortimer Adler, discussing the ideas of justice, liberty and equality, argued for the sovereignty of justice:

> ... we must note the sovereignty of justice. It regulates our thinking about liberty and equality. Without its guidance, certain errors are unavoidable and certain problems insoluble.
>
> ... (J)ustice is the supreme value, a greater good than either liberty or equality, and one that must be appealed to for the rectification of errors with regard to liberty and equality.[23]

He continued:

> Only justice is an unlimited good... One can want too much liberty and too much equality – more than is good for us to have in relation to our fellowmen, and more than we have any right to. Not so with justice. No society can be too just; no individual can act more justly than is good for him or his fellowmen.[24]

Justice, Amartya Sen wrote in his seminal work on this topic, can best be approached as prevention of grievances and inequities. This may be considered a structural approach to the achievement of justice. In this section we shall elucidate the principle of justice as it emerges from the jurisprudence and practice of the monitoring bodies. As we shall see, international human rights law in general and international human rights treaty law in particular, strive for the achievement of just societies grounded in international human rights norms.

Human rights treaty organs strive for equitable balances between the State and the individual in relation to, for example, the balance to be struck between security and freedom. Human rights treaty regimes strive for just satisfaction in instances where it has been established that a violation of human rights has taken place. Article 41 of the European Convention on Human Rights specifically invokes the principle of just satisfaction.

Furthermore, human rights treaty organs apply the concept of the living law, namely that the provisions of treaties will be interpreted and applied in light of the circumstances prevailing at the time of decision on an application, not necessarily the time when the treaty provision was drafted or at the time when an earlier decision was handed down. The Judge case before

---

23 Adler, *Six Great Ideas* (Macmillan Publishing, 1981), pp. 135–136.

24 *Ibid.*, 137.

the Human Rights Committee brought this point out.

4.1 *Striving for Just Societies Grounded in Human Rights Norms*

There are numerous examples in the practice of human rights treaty bodies when they have found the conduct of State organs or officials contrary to the provisions of the applicable treaty and at variance with sentiments of justice. We take as examples, a sample of cases from the Selected Decisions of the Human Rights Committee, Volume 2, covering the period October 1982 to April 1988.[25]

In a number of cases, the Human Rights Committee held that the victim had not been treated "with humanity and with respect for the inherent dignity of the human person" because, for example, he or she had been kept incommunicado at an unknown place of detention for several months during which time his fate and whereabouts were unknown; because the victim had not been treated in prison humanity and with respect for the inherent dignity of the human person; because while in detention he was not treated with humanity; because the victim had not been treated in prison with dignity and respect for the inherent dignity of the human person; because the victim had not been treated in prison with humanity and with respect for the inherent dignity of the human person; because the victim had been kept in solitary confinement for several month in conditions which failed to respect the inherent dignity of the human person; because of the inhuman conditions in which the victim had been held at times in prison; because the victim had not been treated with humanity and with respect for the inherent dignity of the human person; because the victim was subjected to torture and not treated in prison with humanity and with respect for the inherent dignity of the human person, in particular because he was held incommunicado for several months.[26]

In the case of Hiber Conteris, for example, Communication No. 139 /1983, the Human Rights Committee found violations of the International Covenant on Civil and Political Rights because of the severe ill-treatment which the petitioner suffered during the first three months of detention and the harsh and, at time degrading conditions of his detention since then; because of the manner in which he was arrested and detained, without a warrant, which constituted an arbitrary arrest and detention; because

25 International Covenant on Civil and Political Rights. Selected Decisions of the Human Rights Committee under the Optional Protocol. Vol. 2. Seventeenth to thirty-second sessions (October 1982–April 1988). UN publication, Sales No. E.89.XIV.1.

26 *Ibid.*, pp. 118, 121, 126, 130, 135, 148, 154, 157, 160.

he was not informed of the charge against him for over two years; because he was not brought before a judge and because he was not tried within a reasonable time; because he had no opportunity to challenge his detention; because he was held incommunicado for over three months; because he had no fair and public hearing; because he had no effective access to legal counsel for the preparation of his defence; because he was not tried without undue delay; because he was not tried in his presence and could not defend himself in person or through legal counsel of his own choosing; and because he was forced by means of torture to confess guilt. The Human Rights Committee held that the respondent State party, Uruguay, was under an obligation to take effective measures to remedy the violations which Mr Hiber Conteris had suffered and to grant him compensation.[27]

In another case, involving Surinam, the Human Rights Committee found that the victims had been arbitrarily deprived of their lives and urged the State party to take effective steps to investigate the killings, to bring to justice any persons found to be responsible for the deaths of the victims, to pay compensation to the surviving families and to ensure that the right to life is duly protected in Surinam.[28]

In the case of Elena Quinteros Almeida, in which Uruguay was the respondent, the Human Rights Committee held that a mother had the right to know what had happened to her daughter, who had disappeared. The Committee understood the anguish and stress caused to the mother by the disappearance of her daughter And by the continuing uncertainty concerning her fate and whereabouts.[29] In the case of Jose Herrera and Emma Rubia de Herrera, the Human Rights Committee held that Columbia had failed to take appropriate measures to prevent the disappearance and subsequent killings of the victims and to investigate effectively the responsibility for their murders. The Committee referred to its General Comment No. 6 which had provided that States parties should take specific and effective measures to prevent the disappearance of individuals and establish effective facilities and procedures to investigate thoroughly, by an appropriate impartial body, cases of missing and disappeared persons in circumstances that may involve a violation of the right to life.[30]

In the Case of Monja Jaona, in which Madagascar was the respondent, the Human Rights Committee held that the victim had been detained on account of his political opinions and had suffered persecution on account

27 *Ibid.*, p. 171.
28 *Ibid.*, p. 176.
29 *Ibid.*, p. 142.
30 *Ibid.*, p. 195.

of his political opinions.[31] In the case of Lucia Arzuaga Gilboa, in which Uruguay was the respondent, the Human Rights Committee held that the victim had been subjected to torture and to cruel and degrading treatment and had been subjected to inhuman prison conditions for 14 months.[32] The Human Rights Committee made similar findings in the case of Raul Cariboni, in which Uruguay was again the respondent.[33]

One can find cases similar to these in the practice of all of the human rights treaty bodies that examine petitions. The point we seek to make in this sample is that the monitoring organs endeavour to guide the States parties to justice on the basis of the human rights treaty provisions involved. We may also see instances of equitable balances between the State and the individual.

5 Equitable Balances between the State and the Individual

In the case of David Alberto Campora Schweizer, the Human Rights Committee was faced with a regime of 'prompt security measures' in Uruguay. While indicating that it did not feel that it was in a position to pronounce itself on the general compatibility of the regime of prompt security measures under Uruguayan law with the ICCPR, the Committee held that the modalities under which the prompt security measures were ordered, maintained and enforced did not comply with the requirements of Article 9 of the Covenant. It held that there had been violations of Article 9(3) and (4) of the Covenant because, during the time spent in detention under the regime of prompt security measures the victim had not been brought before a judge and could not take proceedings to challenge his arrest and detention.[34]

In the case of Eric Hammel, the Human Rights Committee held that the victim had not been an effective remedy to challenge his expulsion from Madagascar "and that the State party has not shown that there were compelling reasons of national security to deprive him of that remedy."[35]

In a series of cases, the Human Rights Committee held that as a matter of justice, the burden of proof of allegations of violations rested not only on the petitioner but passed to the State party as well. As the Committee has stated:

31 *Ibid.*, p. 164.
32 *Ibid.*, p. 178.
33 *Ibid.*, p. 189.
34 *Ibid.*, p. 93.
35 *Ibid.*, p. 182.

> With regard to the burden of proof… the said burden cannot rest on the author of the communication alone, especially considering that the author and the State party do not always have equal access to the evidence, and that frequently the State party alone has access to relevant information. It is implicit in article 4(2) of the Optional Protocol that the State party has the duty to investigate in good faith all allegations of violation of the [ICCPR] made against it and its authorities, and to furnish to the Committee the information available to it.[36]

6 Survival and Livelihood Rights

Humanity is now in an era in which the very survival of the earth and its inhabitants is at great risk, and in which the right to livelihood is absent for large parts of the population of the planet. The era we are living in calls for dramatic transformations in the structure and content of international law, which must now be geared towards safeguarding and implementing survival and livelihood rights.

In a preceding chapter we argued that the roots of universal rights lay in humanity and that people must now be counted among the sources of evidence of the norms of international law. From this perspective, it is clear that the peoples of the world support and empower survival and livelihood rights as universal rights, notably, the right to a safe environment, the right to life, the right to peace, and the right to development.

7 Conclusion

In this chapter we have sought to present some key concepts: the prevention of violations of human rights, the concept of protection, the idea of equality, the idea of justice, and the emergence of international norms pertinent to the survival of human beings on earth. The reasoning behind this chapter is that judges and lawyers might bear some of these ideas and the relevant practice during the discharge of their duties as guardians of the rule of law.

36 *Ibid.*, p. 86. See, similarly, pp. 86, 108, 116, 120, 187, 188.

10 Conclusion A Judicial and Legal Pledge for Human Rights

The insights shared in this book can be encapsulated in the following Pledge for Human Rights by Judges and Lawyers:

1. I shall always have in view the need for an adequate and effective national human rights protection system in my country and how it might be enhanced.
2. I shall be mindful of the legal obligations undertaken by the Government of my country under the United Nations Charter to uphold human rights at home, without discrimination, and to cooperate with the United Nations for their realization and protection world-wide for everyone, without discrimination.
3. I shall do my part for the faithful implementation of the international and regional human rights treaties that are binding on my country, and for the implementation of rules of international customary law, especially fundamental principles of international public law (*jus cogens*).
4. In seeking to render and uphold justice in the performance of my duties I shall have in view the UN Basic Principles and Guidelines on the Right to a Remedy and Reparation for Victims of Gross Violations of International Human Rights Law and Serious Violations of International Humanitarian Law.
5. I shall support and uphold the UN Basic Principles on the Independence of the Judiciary.
6. I shall have in view always the Universally-Binding Human Rights Norms and I shall play my part in upholding them nationally, regionally, and internationally.
7. I shall do my part to bring to life the legal obligations of the Government of my country to 'prevent human rights violations', to 'respect' human rights, to 'ensure' human rights, to 'fulfil' human rights, to 'guarantee' human rights, and to 'protect' human rights in accordance with the internationally agreed definitions of these terms.
8. I shall always have in view the need to promote and to protect the human rights to dignity, equality, and survival in a world of constant changes and challenges.
9. I shall take inspiration from the historic mission and philosophy

of the International Bill of Rights, which consists of the Universal Declaration of Human Rights, the International Covenant on Economic, Social and Cultural Rights and its Optional Protocol, and the International Covenant on Civil and Political Rights and its Optional Protocols.

10 I shall strive to play my part and to contribute to the promotion and protection of human rights universally.

Appendix 1

A Recapitulation of Core Universally-binding Human Rights

1 Introduction

Universally-binding norms of human rights exist and are applicable to every State in the world. This recapitulation of core universally-binding human rights norms is based on the International Bill of Rights, which consists of the Universal Declaration of Human Rights (1948), the International Covenant on Economic, Social and Cultural Rights (1966), the International Covenant on Civil and Political Rights, and its Optional Protocol (1966).

We have drawn mainly on the Universal Declaration and the corresponding articles of the International Covenant on Civil and Political Rights, especially those from which no derogation is permissible under Article 4 of the Covenant. In formulating the universally-binding rights below we have used the Universal Declaration of Human Rights as the base. We have included most of the rights in the Universal Declaration which, in our judgment, are indispensable rights that have gained the status of international customary law. We have left out some rights in the Universal Declaration that we think have not attained this status.

In three instances, we have elaborated on rights in the Universal Declaration by drawing on three widely ratified international conventions corresponding to those rights: the rights of the child, the rights of women, and the prohibition of against racial discrimination.

When formulating the *jus cogens* rights presented below, we have drawn on the relevant international conventions: the Convention against Genocide;[1] the Convention against Torture; the Convention against *Apartheid;*[2] and, in respect of the right of self-determination, the opening article of the two international covenants. In relation to the prohibition of slavery, the relevant international conventions are quite complex and we have, for the time being, kept to the provisions of the Universal Declaration and the International Covenant on Civil and Political Rights.

Because of the progressive nature of the rights in the International Covenant on Economic, Social and Cultural Rights (other than the right to non-discrimination, which is of immediate application) we have not

1 Convention on the Prevention and Punishment of the Crime of Genocide. Paris, 1948. 78 UNTS 277.

2 International Convention on the Suppression and Punishment of the Crime of Apartheid. New York, 1973. 1015 UNTS 243.

sought to identify universally binding human rights norms from this Covenant. Such an exercise might be tackled in a future endeavour.

There are undoubtedly more universally-binding human rights that could be added to the list below. This recapitulation is intended as a start to the process of identifying universally binding human rights norms.

2 The Sources of Universally-binding Human Rights Norms

The sources of universally-binding human rights norms are international customary law, including norms of *jus cogens*; universally ratified treaties such as the UN Charter and the Convention on the Rights of the Child; treaty norms that have evolved into international customary law, such as the non-derogable rights under Article 4 of the ICCPR; rights in UN declarations that have matured into international customary law; rights deriving from general principles of law; and rights contained in authoritative statements of representative peoples' assemblies.

3 The Universal Periodic Review (UPR)

The Universal Periodic Review operated by the UN Human Rights Council helps promote the universal realization of human rights. The bases of the review, as mandated by the UN General Assembly, include the UN Charter, the Universal Declaration of Human Rights, human rights instruments to which a State is party, and voluntary pledges and commitments made by States. The practice of States under the UPR process may be drawn upon to support the formation of international customary law on the basis of some rights contained in the Universal Declaration.

4 Universally-binding Obligations Under the UN Charter

Under the UN Charter, every Government is legally obliged to have in place an adequate and effective national human rights protection system and to cooperate with the UN for the universal realization and protection of human rights.

5 *Jus cogens* rights

Universally binding *jus cogens* rights include: the prohibition of genocide, slavery, torture, and apartheid; and the right of self-determination.

A *Prohibition of Genocide*

Genocide, whether committed in time of peace or in time of war, is a crime under international law which Governments undertake to prevent and to punish. (Genocide Convention, Article I).

Genocide means any of the following acts committed with intent to destroy, in whole or in part, a national, ethnical, racial or religious group, as such:

(a) Killing members of the group;
(b) Causing serious bodily or mental harm to members of the group;
(c) Deliberately inflicting on the group conditions of life calculated to bring about its physical destruction in whole or in part;
(d) Imposing measures intended to prevent births within the group;
(e) Forcibly transferring children of the group to another group (Genocide Convention, Article II).

The following acts are punishable:

(a) Genocide;
(b) Conspiracy to commit genocide;
(c) Direct and public incitement to commit genocide;
(d) Attempt to commit genocide;
(e) Complicity in genocide (Genocide Convention, Article III).

Persons committing genocide or any of the other acts enumerated in article III shall be punished, whether they are constitutionally responsible rulers, public officials or private individuals (Genocide Convention, Article IV).

B *Prohibition of Slavery*

No-one shall be held in slavery or servitude; slavery and the slave trade shall be prohibited in all their forms (UDHR, Article 4).

No-one shall be held in slavery; slavery and the slave-trade in all their forms shall be prohibited. No-one shall be held in servitude (ICCPR, Article 4).

C *Prohibition of Torture*

No-one shall be subjected to torture or to cruel, inhuman or degrading treatment or punishment (UDHR, Article 5).

No-one shall be subjected without his free consent to medical or scientific experimentation (ICCPR, Article 7).

Torture means any act by which severe pain or suffering, whether physical or mental, is intentionally inflicted on a person for such purposes as obtaining from him or a third person information or a confession, punishing him for an act he or a third person has committed or is suspected of having committed, or intimidating or coercing him or a third person, or for any reason based on discrimination of any kind, when such pain or suffering is inflicted by or at the instigation of or with the consent or acquiescence of a public official or other person acting in an official capacity. It does not include pain or suffering arising only from, inherent in or incidental to lawful sanctions (Convention against Torture (CAT), Article 1).

1. Each State Party shall take effective legislative, administrative, judicial or other measures to prevent acts of torture in any territory under its jurisdiction.
2. No exceptional circumstances whatsoever, whether a state of war or a threat of war, internal political instability or any other public emergency, may be invoked as a justification of torture.
3. An order from a superior officer or a public authority may not be invoked as a justification of torture (CAT, Article 2).

D *Prohibition of Apartheid*

Apartheid is a crime against humanity and that inhuman acts resulting from the policies and practices of apartheid and similar policies and practices of racial segregation and discrimination, as defined in article II of the Convention, are crimes violating the principles of international law, in particular the purposes and principles of the Charter of the United Nations, and constituting a serious threat to international peace and security (Convention against *Apartheid,* Article I).

The term 'the crime of apartheid' includes similar policies and practices of racial segregation and discrimination as practised in southern Africa by the former *apartheid* regime, and includes the following inhuman acts committed for the purpose of establishing and maintaining domination by one racial group of persons over any other racial group of persons and systematically oppressing them:

(a) Denial to a member or members of a racial group or groups of the right to life and liberty of person:
(i) By murder of members of a racial group or groups;
(ii) By the infliction upon the members of a racial group or groups of serious bodily or mental harm, by the infringement of their freedom or dignity, or by subjecting them to torture or to cruel, inhuman or degrading treatment or punishment;
(iii) By arbitrary arrest and illegal imprisonment of the members of a racial group or groups;
(b) Deliberate imposition on a racial group or groups of living conditions calculated to cause its or their physical destruction in whole or in part;

(c) Any legislative measures and other measures calculated to prevent a racial group or groups from participation in the political, social, economic and cultural life of the country and the deliberate creation of conditions preventing the full development of such a group or groups, in particular by denying to members of a racial group or groups basic human rights and freedoms, including the right to work, the right to form recognized trade unions, the right to education, the right to leave and to return to their country, the right to a nationality, the right to freedom of movement and residence, the right to freedom of opinion and expression, and the right to freedom of peaceful assembly and association;
(d) Any measures including legislative measures, designed to divide the population along racial lines by the creation of separate reserves and ghettos for the members of a racial group or groups, the prohibition of mixed marriages among members of various racial groups, the expropriation of landed property belonging to a racial group or groups or to members thereof;
(e) Exploitation of the labour of the members of a racial group or groups, in particular by submitting them to forced labour;
(f) Persecution of organizations and persons, by depriving them of fundamental rights and freedoms, because they oppose apartheid (Convention against *Apartheid*, Article II).

International criminal responsibility shall apply, irrespective of the motive involved, to individuals, members of organizations and institutions and representatives of the State, whether residing in the territory of the State in which the acts are perpetrated or in some other State, whenever they:
(a) Commit, participate in, directly incite or conspire in the commission of the crime of *apartheid.*
(b) Directly abet, encourage or co-operate in the commission of the crime of apartheid (International Convention against *Apartheid*, Article III).

E *Right of Self-determination*

All peoples have the right of self-determination. By virtue of that right they freely determine their political status and freely pursue their economic, social and cultural development.

All peoples may, for their own ends, freely dispose of their natural wealth and resources without prejudice to any obligations arising out of international economic co-operation, based upon the principle of mutual benefit, and international law. In no case may a people be deprived of its own means of subsistence (Article 1 of both ICCPR and ICESCR).

6 Core Universally-binding Human Rights

Universally-binding human rights may be identified in the UN Charter, the Universal Declaration of Human Rights, the International Covenants on human rights, the Convention on the Rights of the Child, the Convention on the Elimination of Discrimination against Women, the Convention on the Elimination of Racial Discrimination, and other treaties. Universally-binding human rights include:

A *The Right to Life*

Everyone has the right to life, liberty and the security of person (UDHR, Article 3).

Every human being has the inherent right to life. This right shall be protected by law. No one shall be arbitrarily deprived of his life (ICCPR, Article 6).

B *The Right to a Clean, Healthy and Sustainable Environment*

The General Assembly, "1. *Recognizes* the right to a clean, healthy and sustainable environment as a human right" (GA Resolution A/Res/76/300).

C *The Right to Dignity*

All human beings are born free and equal in dignity and rights. They are endowed with reason and conscience and should act towards one another in a spirit of brotherhood (UDHR, Article 1).

D *The Right to Liberty and Security of Person*

Everyone has the right to life, liberty and the security of person (UDHR, Article 3).

E *The Right to Equality and Non-discrimination*

All are equal before the law and are entitled without any discrimination to equal protection of the law. All are entitled to equal protection against any discrimination in violation of this Declaration and against any incitement to such discrimination (UDHR, Article 7).

Everyone is entitled to all internationally recognized rights and freedoms without distinction of any kind, such as race, colour, sex, language, religion, political or other opinion, national or social origin, property, birth or other status. Furthermore, no distinction shall be made on the basis of the political, jurisdictional or international status of the country or territory to which a person belongs, whether it be independent, trust, non-self-governing or under any other limitation of sovereignty (UDHR, Article 2).

Racial discrimination is unlawful in international law. Racial discrimination means any distinction, exclusion, restriction or preference based on race, colour, descent, or national or ethnic origin which has the purpose or effect of nullifying or impairing the recognition, enjoyment or exercise, on an equal footing, of human rights and fundamental freedoms in the political, economic, social, cultural or any other field of public life (CERD, Article 1).

Every Government shall take effective measures to review governmental, national and local policies, and to amend, rescind or nullify any laws and regulations which have the effect of creating or perpetuating racial discrimination wherever it exists. Every Government shall prohibit and bring to an end, by all appropriate means, including legislation as required by circumstances, racial discrimination by any persons, group or organization (CERD, Article 2).

Every Government shall assure to everyone within their jurisdiction effective protection and remedies, through the competent national tribunals and other State institutions, against any acts of racial discrimination which violate his human rights and fundamental freedoms contrary to this Convention, as well as the right to seek from such tribunals just and adequate reparation or satisfaction for any damage suffered as a result of such discrimination (CERD, Article 6).

F *The Right to Recognition Everywhere as a Person Before the Law*

Everyone has the right to recognition everywhere as a person before the law (UDHR, Article 6).

G *The Rights of the Child*

A child means every human being below the age of eighteen years unless under the law applicable to the child, majority is attained earlier (CRC, Article 1).

Every Government shall respect and ensure the rights set forth in the present Convention to each child within their jurisdiction without discrimination of any kind, irrespective of the child's or his or her parent's or legal guardian's race, colour, sex, language, religion, political or other opinion, national, ethnic or social origin, property, disability, birth or other status. Every Government shall take all appropriate measures to ensure that the child is protected against all forms of discrimination or punishment on the basis of the status, activities, expressed opinions, or beliefs of the child's parents, legal guardians, or family members (CRC, Article 2).

In all actions concerning children, whether undertaken by public or private social welfare institutions, courts of law, administrative authorities or legislative bodies, the best interests of the child shall be a primary consideration. Every Government shall ensure the child such protection and care as is necessary for his or her well-being, taking into account the rights and duties of his or her parents, legal guardians, or other individuals legally responsible for him or her, and, to this end, shall take all appropriate legislative and administrative measures Every Government shall ensure that the institutions, services and facilities responsible for the care or protection of children shall conform with the standards established by competent authorities, particularly in the areas of safety, health, in the number and suitability of their staff, as well as competent supervision (CRC, Article 3).

Every Government shall undertake to have respect for the liberty of parents and, when applicable, legal guardians to ensure the religious and moral education of their children in conformity with their own convictions (CRC, Article 4).

H *The Rights of Women*

Every Government shall condemn discrimination against women in all its forms, agree to pursue by all appropriate means and without delay a policy of eliminating discrimination against women and, to this end, undertake:

(a) To embody the principle of the equality of men and women in their national constitutions or other appropriate legislation if not yet incorporated therein and to ensure, through law and other appropriate means, the practical realization of this principle;
(b) To adopt appropriate legislative and other measures, including sanctions where appropriate, prohibiting all discrimination against women;
(c) To establish legal protection of the rights of women on an equal basis with men and to ensure through competent national tribunals and other public institutions the effective protection of women against any act of discrimination;
(d) To refrain from engaging in any act or practice of discrimination against women and to ensure that public authorities and institutions shall act in conformity with this obligation;
(e) To take all appropriate measures to eliminate discrimination against women by any person, organization or enterprise;
(f) To take all appropriate measures, including legislation, to modify or abolish existing laws, regulations, customs and practices which constitute discrimination against women;
(g) To repeal all national penal provisions which constitute discrimination against women.

The term "discrimination against women" means any distinction, exclusion or restriction made on the basis of sex which has the effect or purpose of impairing or nullifying the recognition, enjoyment or exercise by women, irrespective of their marital status, on a basis of equality of men and women, of human rights and fundamental freedoms in the political, economic, social, cultural, civil or any other field (CEDAW, Article 1).

Every Government shall take in all fields, in particular in the political, social, economic and cultural fields, all appropriate measures, including legislation, to en sure the full development and advancement of women, for the purpose of guaranteeing them the exercise and enjoyment of human rights and fundamental freedoms on a basis of equality with men (CEDAW, Article 3).

I *The Right to an Effective Remedy*

Everyone has the right to an effective remedy by the competent national tribunals for acts violating the fundamental rights granted him by the constitution or by law (UDHR, Article 8).

J *Protection from Arbitrary Arrest, Detention or Exile*

No one shall be subjected to arbitrary arrest, detention or exile (UDHR, Article 9).

K *The Right to a Fair and Public Hearing by an Independent and Impartial Tribunal*

Everyone is entitled in full equality to a fair and public hearing by an independent and impartial tribunal, in the determination of his rights and obligations and of any criminal charge against him (UDHR, Article 10).

L *The Right to be Presumed Innocent Until Proved Guilty According to Law*

Everyone charged with a penal offence has the right to be presumed innocent until proved guilty according to law in a public trial at which he has had all the guarantees necessary for his defence.

No-one shall be held guilty of any penal offence on account of any act or omission which did not constitute a penal offence, under national or international law, at the time when it was committed. Nor shall a heavier penalty be imposed than the one that was applicable at the time the penal offence was committed (UDHR, Article 11).

M *The Right to be Protected from Arbitrary Interference with One's Privacy, Family, Home or Correspondence*

No one shall be subjected to arbitrary interference with his privacy, family, home or correspondence, nor to attacks upon his honour and reputation. Everyone has the right to the protection of the law against such interference or attacks (UDHR, Article 12).

N *The Right to Freedom of Movement and Residence within the Borders of Each State*

Everyone has the right to freedom of movement and residence within the borders of each State. Everyone has the right to leave any country, including his own, and to return to his country (UDHR, Article 13).

O *The Right to Seek and to Enjoy in Other Countries Asylum from Persecution*

Everyone has the right to seek and to enjoy in other countries asylum from persecution (UDHR, Article 14).

P *The Right to a Nationality*

Everyone has the right to a nationality. No one shall be arbitrarily deprived of his nationality nor denied the right to change his nationality (UDHR, Article 15).

Q *Protection of the Family and of the Right to Marry and to Found a Family*

The family is the natural and fundamental group unit of society and is entitled to protection by society and the State. Men and women of full age, without any limitation due to race, nationality or religion, have the right to marry and to found a family. They are entitled to equal rights as to marriage, during marriage and at its dissolution. Marriage shall be entered into only with the free and full consent of the intending spouses (UDHR, Article 16).

R *The Right to Freedom of Thought, Conscience and Religion*

Everyone has the right to freedom of thought, conscience and religion; this right includes freedom to change his religion or belief, and freedom, either alone or in community with others and in public or private, to manifest his religion or belief in teaching, practice, worship and observance (UDHR, Article 18).

Everyone shall have the right to freedom of thought, conscience and religion. This right shall include freedom to have or to adopt a religion or belief of his choice, and freedom, either individually or in community with others and in public or private, to manifest his religion or belief in worship, observance, practice and teaching.

No-one shall be subject to coercion which would impair his freedom to have or to adopt a religion or belief of his choice.

Freedom to manifest one's religion or beliefs may be subject only to such limitations as are prescribed by law and are necessary to protect public safety, order, health, or morals or the fundamental rights and freedoms of others (ICCPR, Article 18).

S *The Right to Freedom of Opinion and Expression*

Everyone has the right to freedom of opinion and expression; this right includes freedom to hold opinions without interference and to seek, receive and impart information and ideas through any media and regardless of frontiers (UDHR, Article 19).

T *The Right to Freedom of Peaceful Assembly and Association*

Everyone has the right to freedom of peaceful assembly and association. No one may be compelled to belong to an association (UDHR, Article 20).

U *The Right to Take Part in the Government of One's Country, Directly or through Freely Chosen Representatives*

Everyone has the right to take part in the government of his country, directly or through freely chosen representatives. Everyone has the right of equal access to public service in his country. The will of the people shall be the basis of the authority of government; this will shall be expressed in periodic and genuine elections which shall be by universal and equal suffrage and shall be held by secret vote or by equivalent free voting procedures (UDHR, Article 21).

V *The Right to Education*

Everyone has the right to education. Education shall be free, at least in the elementary and fundamental stages. Elementary education shall be compulsory. Technical and professional education shall be made generally available and higher education shall be equally accessible to all on the basis of merit (UDHR, Article 26).

W *The Right to Social Security*

Everyone, as a member of society, has the right to social security and is entitled to realization, through national effort and international co-operation and in accordance with the organization and resources of each State, of the economic, social and cultural rights indispensable for his dignity and the free development of his personality (UDHR, Article 22).

X *Cultural Rights*

Everyone has the right freely to participate in the cultural life of the community, to enjoy the arts and to share in scientific advancement and its benefits. Everyone has the right to the protection of the moral and material interests resulting from any scientific, literary or artistic production of which he is the author (UDHR, Article 27).

Y *The Right to Property*

Everyone has the right to own property alone as well as in association with others. No one shall be arbitrarily deprived of his property (UDHR, Article 17).

Z *Universal Norms of International Humanitarian Law*

Universally-binding rules of International Humanitarian Law have been documented by the ICRC in its study on Customary International Humanitarian Law.[3]

3 The International Committee of the Red Cross, *Customary International Humanitarian Law,* by Jean-Marie Henckaerts and Louise Doswald-Beck (Cambridge, Cambridge University Press, 2005).

Appendix 2
The International Bill of Human Rights

1 The Universal Declaration of Human Rights
Adopted and Proclaimed by General Assembly Resolution 217 A (III) of 10 December 1948

Preamble

Whereas recognition of the inherent dignity and of the equal and inalienable rights of all members of the human family is the foundation of freedom, justice and peace in the world,

Whereas disregard and contempt for human rights have resulted in barbarous acts which have outraged the conscience of mankind, and the advent of a world in which human beings shall enjoy freedom of speech and belief and freedom from fear and want has been proclaimed as the highest aspiration of the common people,

Whereas it is essential, if man is not to be compelled to have recourse, as a last resort, to rebellion against tyranny and oppression, that human rights should be protected by the rule of law,

Whereas it is essential to promote the development of friendly relations between nations,

Whereas the peoples of the United Nations have in the Charter reaffirmed their faith in fundamental human rights, in the dignity and worth of the human person and in the equal rights of men and women and have determined to promote social progress and better standards of life in larger freedom,

Whereas Member States have pledged themselves to achieve, in co-operation with the United Nations, the promotion of universal respect for and observance of human rights and fundamental freedoms,

Whereas a common understanding of these rights and freedoms is of the greatest importance for the full realization of this pledge,

Now, therefore, The General Assembly,

Proclaims this Universal Declaration of Human Rights as a common standard of achievement for all peoples and all nations, to the end that every individual and every organ of society, keeping this Declaration constantly in mind, shall strive by teaching and education to promote respect for these rights and freedoms and by progressive measures, national and international, to secure their universal and effective recognition and observance, both among the peoples of Member States themselves and among the peoples of territories under their jurisdiction.

Article 1

All human beings are born free and equal in dignity and rights. They are endowed with reason and conscience and should act towards one another in a spirit of brotherhood.

Article 2

Everyone is entitled to all the rights and freedoms set forth in this Declaration, without distinction of any kind, such as race, colour, sex, language, religion, political or other opinion, national or social origin, property, birth or other status.

Furthermore, no distinction shall be made on the basis of the political, jurisdictional or international status of the country or territory to which a person belongs, whether it be independent, trust, non-self-governing or under any other limitation of sovereignty.

Article 3

Everyone has the right to life, liberty and security of person.

Article 4

No one shall be held in slavery or servitude; slavery and the slave trade shall be prohibited in all their forms.

Article 5

No one shall be subjected to torture or to cruel, inhuman or degrading treatment or punishment.

Article 6

Everyone has the right to recognition everywhere as a person before the law.

Article 7

All are equal before the law and are entitled without any discrimination to equal protection of the law. All are entitled to equal protection against any discrimination in violation of this Declaration and against any incitement to such discrimination.

Article 8

Everyone has the right to an effective remedy by the competent national tribunals for acts violating the fundamental rights granted him by the constitution or by law.

Article 9

No one shall be subjected to arbitrary arrest, detention or exile.

Article 10

Everyone is entitled in full equality to a fair and public hearing by an independent and impartial tribunal, in the determination of his rights and obligations and of any criminal charge against him.

Article 11

1. Everyone charged with a penal offence has the right to be presumed innocent until proved guilty according to law in a public trial at which he has had all the guarantees necessary for his defence.
2. No one shall be held guilty of any penal offence on account of any act or omission which did not constitute a penal offence, under national or international law, at the time when it was committed. Nor shall a heavier penalty be imposed than the one that was applicable at the time the penal offence was committed.

Article 12

No one shall be subjected to arbitrary interference with his privacy, family, home or correspondence, nor to attacks upon his honour and reputation. Everyone has the right to the protection of the law against such interference or attacks.

Article 13

1. Everyone has the right to freedom of movement and residence within the borders of each State.
2. Everyone has the right to leave any country, including his own, and to return to his country.

Article 14

1. Everyone has the right to seek and to enjoy in other countries asylum from persecution.
2. This right may not be invoked in the case of prosecutions genuinely arising from non-political crimes or from acts contrary to the purposes and principles of the United Nations.

Article 15

1. Everyone has the right to a nationality.
2. No one shall be arbitrarily deprived of his nationality nor denied the right to change his nationality.

Article 16

1. Men and women of full age, without any limitation due to race, nationality or religion, have the right to marry and to found a family. They are entitled to equal rights as to marriage, during marriage and at its dissolution.
2. Marriage shall be entered into only with the free and full consent of the intending spouses.
3. The family is the natural and fundamental group unit of society and is entitled to protection by society and the State.

Article 17

1. Everyone has the right to own property alone as well as in association with others.
2. No one shall be arbitrarily deprived of his property.

Article 18

Everyone has the right to freedom of thought, conscience and religion; this right includes freedom to change his religion or belief, and freedom, either alone or in community with others and in public or private, to manifest his religion or belief in teaching, practice, worship and observance.

Article 19

Everyone has the right to freedom of opinion and expression; this right includes freedom to hold opinions without interference and to seek, receive and impart information and ideas through any media and regardless of frontiers.

Article 20

1. Everyone has the right to freedom of peaceful assembly and association.
2. No one may be compelled to belong to an association.

Article 21

1. Everyone has the right to take part in the government of his country, directly or through freely chosen representatives.
2. Everyone has the right to equal access to public service in his country.
3. The will of the people shall be the basis of the authority of government; this will shall be expressed in periodic and genuine elections which shall be by universal and equal suffrage and shall be held by secret vote or by equivalent free voting procedures.

Article 22

Everyone, as a member of society, has the right to social security and is entitled to realization, through national effort and international co-operation and in accordance with the organization and resources of each State, of the economic, social and cultural rights indispensable for his dignity and the free development of his personality.

Article 23

1. Everyone has the right to work, to free choice of employment, to just and favourable conditions of work and to protection against unemployment.
2. Everyone, without any discrimination, has the right to equal pay for equal work.
3. Everyone who works has the right to just and favourable remuneration ensuring for himself and his family an existence worthy of human dignity, and supplemented, if necessary, by other means of social protection.
4. Everyone has the right to form and to join trade unions for the protection of his interests.

Article 24

Everyone has the right to rest and leisure, including reasonable limitation of working hours and periodic holidays with pay.

Article 25

1. Everyone has the right to a standard of living adequate for the health and well-being of himself and of his family, including food, clothing, housing and medical care and necessary social services, and the right to security in the event of unemployment, sickness, disability, widowhood, old age or other lack of livelihood in circumstances beyond his control.
2. Motherhood and childhood are entitled to special care and assistance. All children, whether born in or out of wedlock, shall enjoy the same social protection.

Article 26

1. Everyone has the right to education. Education shall be free, at least in the elementary and fundamental stages. Elementary education shall be compulsory. Technical and professional education shall be made generally available and higher education shall be equally accessible to all on the basis of merit.
2. Education shall be directed to the full development of the human personality and to the strengthening of respect for human rights and funda-

mental freedoms. It shall promote understanding, tolerance and friendship among all nations, racial or religious groups, and shall further the activities of the United Nations for the maintenance of peace.

3. Parents have a prior right to choose the kind of education that shall be given to their children.

Article 27

1. Everyone has the right freely to participate in the cultural life of the community, to enjoy the arts and to share in scientific advancement and its benefits.

2. Everyone has the right to the protection of the moral and material interests resulting from any scientific, literary or artistic production of which he is the author.

Article 28

Everyone is entitled to a social and international order in which the rights and freedoms set forth in this Declaration can be fully realized.

Article 29

1. Everyone has duties to the community in which alone the free and full development of his personality is possible.

2. In the exercise of his rights and freedoms, everyone shall be subject only to such limitations as are determined by law solely for the purpose of securing due recognition and respect for the rights and freedoms of others and of meeting the just requirements of morality, public order and the general welfare in a democratic society.

3. These rights and freedoms may in no case be exercised contrary to the purposes and principles of the United Nations.

Article 30

Nothing in this Declaration may be interpreted as implying for any State, group or person any right to engage in any activity or to perform any act aimed at the destruction of any of the rights and freedoms set forth herein.

2 The International Covenant on Economic, Social and Cultural Rights

Adopted and Opened for Signature, Ratification and Accession by General Assembly Resolution 2200 A (XXI) of 16 December 1966
Entry into Force: 3 January 1976, in Accordance with Article 27

Preamble

The States Parties to the present Covenant,

Considering that, in accordance with the principles proclaimed in the Charter of the United Nations, recognition of the inherent dignity and of the equal and inalienable rights of all members of the human family is the foundation of freedom, justice and peace in the world,

Recognizing that these rights derive from the inherent dignity of the human person,

Recognizing that, in accordance with the Universal Declaration of Human Rights, the ideal of free human beings enjoying freedom from fear and want can only be achieved if conditions are created whereby everyone may enjoy his economic, social and cultural rights, as well as his civil and political rights,

Considering the obligation of States under the Charter of the United Nations to promote universal respect for, and observance of, human rights and freedoms,

Realizing that the individual, having duties to other individuals and to the community to which he belongs, is under a responsibility to strive for the promotion and observance of the rights recognized in the present Covenant,

Agree upon the following articles:

Part I

Article 1

1. All peoples have the right of self-determination. By virtue of that right they freely determine their political status and freely pursue their economic, social and cultural development.
2. All peoples may, for their own ends, freely dispose of their natural wealth and resources without prejudice to any obligations arising out of international economic co-operation, based upon the principle of mutual benefit, and international law. In no case may a people be deprived of its own means of subsistence.
3. The States Parties to the present Covenant, including those having responsibility for the administration of Non-Self-Governing and Trust Territories, shall promote the realization of the right of self-determination, and

shall respect that right, in conformity with the provisions of the Charter of the United Nations.

Part II

Article 2

1. Each State Party to the present Covenant undertakes to take steps, individually and through international assistance and co-operation, especially economic and technical, to the maximum of its available resources, with a view to achieving progressively the full realization of the rights recognized in the present Covenant by all appropriate means, including particularly the adoption of legislative measures.

2. The States Parties to the present Covenant undertake to guarantee that the rights enunciated in the present Covenant will be exercised without discrimination of any kind as to race, colour, sex, language, religion, political or other opinion, national or social origin, property, birth or other status.

3. Developing countries, with due regard to human rights and their national economy, may determine to what extent they would guarantee the economic rights recognized in the present Covenant to non-nationals.

Article 3

The States Parties to the present Covenant undertake to ensure the equal right of men and women to the enjoyment of all economic, social and cultural rights set forth in the present Covenant.

Article 4

The States Parties to the present Covenant recognize that, in the enjoyment of those rights provided by the State in conformity with the present Covenant, the State may subject such rights only to such limitations as are determined by law only in so far as this may be compatible with the nature of these rights and solely for the purpose of promoting the general welfare in a democratic society.

Article 5

1. Nothing in the present Covenant may be interpreted as implying for any State, group or person any right to engage in any activity or to perform any act aimed at the destruction of any of the rights or freedoms recognized herein, or at their limitation to a greater extent than is provided for in the present Covenant.

2. No restriction upon or derogation from any of the fundamental human rights recognized or existing in any country in virtue of law, conven-

tions, regulations or custom shall be admitted on the pretext that the present Covenant does not recognize such rights or that it recognizes them to a lesser extent.

Part III

Article 6

1. The States Parties to the present Covenant recognize the right to work, which includes the right of everyone to the opportunity to gain his living by work which he freely chooses or accepts, and will take appropriate steps to safeguard this right.
2. The steps to be taken by a State Party to the present Covenant to achieve the full realization of this right shall include technical and vocational guidance and training programmes, policies and techniques to achieve steady economic, social and cultural development and full and productive employment under conditions safeguarding fundamental political and economic freedoms to the individual.

Article 7

The States Parties to the present Covenant recognize the right of everyone to the enjoyment of just and favourable conditions of work which ensure, in particular:

(a) Remuneration which provides all workers, as a minimum, with:

(i) Fair wages and equal remuneration for work of equal value without distinction of any kind, in particular women being guaranteed conditions of work not inferior to those enjoyed by men, with equal pay for equal work;

(ii) A decent living for themselves and their families in accordance with the provisions of the present Covenant;

(b) Safe and healthy working conditions;

(c) Equal opportunity for everyone to be promoted in his employment to an appropriate higher level, subject to no considerations other than those of seniority and competence;

(d) Rest, leisure and reasonable limitation of working hours and periodic holidays with pay, as well as remuneration for public holidays.

Article 8

1. The States Parties to the present Covenant undertake to ensure:

(a) The right of everyone to form trade unions and join the trade union of hischoice, subject only to the rules of the organization concerned, for the promotion and protection of his economic and social interests. No restrictions may be placed on the exercise of this right other than those prescribed by law and which are necessary in a democratic society in the interests of national security or public order or for the protection of the rights and freedoms of others;

(b) The right of trade unions to establish national federations or confederations and the right of the latter to form or join international trade-union organizations;

(c) The right of trade unions to function freely subject to no limitations other than those prescribed by law and which are necessary in a democratic society in the interests of national security or public order or for the protection of the rights and freedoms of others;

(d) The right to strike, provided that it is exercised in conformity with the laws of the particular country.

2. This article shall not prevent the imposition of lawful restrictions on the exercise of these rights by members of the armed forces or of the police or of the administration of the State.

3. Nothing in this article shall authorize States Parties to the International Labour Organisation Convention of 1948 concerning Freedom of Association and Protection of the Right to Organise to take legislative measures which would prejudice, or apply the law in such a manner as would prejudice, the guarantees provided for in that Convention.

Article 9

The States Parties to the present Covenant recognize the right of everyone to social security, including social insurance.

Article 10

1. The States Parties to the present Covenant recognize that:

The widest possible protection and assistance should be accorded to the family, which is the natural and fundamental group unit of society, particularly for its establishment and while it is responsible for the care and education of dependent children. Marriage must be entered into with the free consent of the intending spouses.

2. Special protection should be accorded to mothers during a reasonable period before and after childbirth. During such period working mothers should be accorded paid leave or leave with adequate social security benefits.

3. Special measures of protection and assistance should be taken on behalf of all children and young persons without any discrimination for reasons of parentage or other conditions. Children and young persons should be protected from economic and social exploitation. Their employment in work harmful to their morals or health or dangerous to life or likely

to hamper their normal development should be punishable by law. States should also set age limits below which the paid employment of child labour should be prohibited and punishable by law.

Article 11

1. The States Parties to the present Covenant recognize the right of everyone to an adequate standard of living for himself and his family, including adequate food, clothing and housing, and to the continuous improvement of living conditions. The States Parties will take appropriate steps to ensure the realization of this right, recognizing to this effect the essential importance of international co-operation based on free consent.

2. The States Parties to the present Covenant, recognizing the fundamental right of everyone to be free from hunger, shall take, individually and through international co-operation, the measures, including specific programmes, which are needed:

(a) To improve methods of production, conservation and distribution of food by making full use of technical and scientific knowledge, by disseminating knowledge of the principles of nutrition and by developing or reforming agrarian systems in such a way as to achieve the most efficient development and utilization of natural resources;

(b) Taking into account the problems of both food-importing and foodexporting countries, to ensure an equitable distribution of world food supplies in relation to need.

Article 12

1. The States Parties to the present Covenant recognize the right of everyone to the enjoyment of the highest attainable standard of physical and mental health.

2. The steps to be taken by the States Parties to the present Covenant to achieve the full realization of this right shall include those necessary for:

(a) The provision for the reduction of the stillbirth-rate and of infant mortality and for the healthy development of the child;

(b) The improvement of all aspects of environmental and industrial hygiene;

(c) The prevention, treatment and control of epidemic, endemic, occupational and other diseases;

(d) The creation of conditions which would assure to all medical service and medical attention in the event of sickness.

Article 13

1. The States Parties to the present Covenant recognize the right of everyone to education. They agree that education shall be directed to the full development of the human personality and the sense of its dignity, and shall strengthen the respect for human rights and fundamental freedoms. They further agree that education shall enable all persons to participate effectively in a free society, promote understanding, tolerance and friendship among all nations and all racial, ethnic or religious groups, and further the activities of the United Nations for the maintenance of peace.

2. The States Parties to the present Covenant recognize that, with a view to achieving the full realization of this right:

(a) Primary education shall be compulsory and available free to all;

(b) Secondary education in its different forms, including technical and vocational secondary education, shall be made generally available and accessible to all by every appropriate means, and in particular by the progressive introduction of free education;

(c) Higher education shall be made equally accessible to all, on the basis of capacity, by every appropriate means, and in particular by the progressive introduction of free education;

(d) Fundamental education shall be encouraged or intensified as far as possible for those persons who have not received or completed the whole period of their primary education;

(e) The development of a system of schools at all levels shall be actively pursued, an adequate fellowship system shall be established, and the material conditions of teaching staff shall be continuously improved.

3. The States Parties to the present Covenant undertake to have respect for the liberty of parents and, when applicable, legal guardians to choose for their children schools, other than those established by the public authorities, which conform to such minimum educational standards as may be laid down or approved by the State and to ensure the religious and moral education of their children in conformity with their own convictions.

4. No part of this article shall be construed so as to interfere with the liberty of individuals and bodies to establish and direct educational institutions, subject always to the observance of the principles set forth in paragraph 1 of this article and to the requirement that the education given in such institutions shall conform to such minimum standards as may be laid down by the State.

Article 14

Each State Party to the present Covenant which, at the time of becoming a Party, has not been able to secure in its metropolitan territory or other territories under its jurisdiction compulsory primary education, free of charge, undertakes, within two years, to work out and adopt a detailed plan of action for the progressive implementation, within a reasonable number of years, to be fixed in the plan, of the principle of compulsory education free of charge for all.

Article 15

1. The States Parties to the present Covenant recognize the right of everyone:

(a) To take part in cultural life;

(b) To enjoy the benefits of scientific progress and its applications;

(c) To benefit from the protection of the moral and material interests resulting from any scientific, literary or artistic production of which he is the author.

2. The steps to be taken by the States Parties to the present Covenant to achieve the full realization of this right shall include those necessary for the conservation, the development and the diffusion of science and culture.

3. The States Parties to the present Covenant undertake to respect the freedom indispensable for scientific research and creative activity.

4. The States Parties to the present Covenant recognize the benefits to be derived from the encouragement and development of international contacts and cooperation in the scientific and cultural fields.

Part IV

Article 16

1. The States Parties to the present Covenant undertake to submit in conformity with this part of the Covenant reports on the measures which they have adopted and the progress made in achieving the observance of the rights recognized herein.

2.(a) All reports shall be submitted to the Secretary-General of the United Nations, who shall transmit copies to the Economic and Social Council for consideration in accordance with the provisions of the present Covenant;

(b) The Secretary-General of the United Nations shall also transmit to the specialized agencies copies of the reports, or any relevant parts therefrom, from States Parties to the present Covenant which are also members of these specialized agencies in so far as these reports, or parts therefrom, relate to any matters which fall within the responsibilities of the said agencies in accordance with their constitutional instruments.

Article 17

1. The States Parties to the present Covenant shall furnish their reports in stages, in accordance with a programme to be established by the Economic and Social Council within one year of the entry into force of the present Covenant after consultation with the States Parties and the specialized agencies concerned.

2. Reports may indicate factors and difficulties affecting the degree of fulfilment of obligations under the present Covenant.

3. Where relevant information has previously been furnished to the United Nations or to any specialized agency by any State Party to the present Covenant, it will not be necessary to reproduce that information, but a precise reference to the information so furnished will suffice.

Article 18

Pursuant to its responsibilities under the Charter of the United Nations in the field of human rights and fundamental freedoms, the Economic and Social Council may make arrangements with the specialized agencies in respect of their reporting to it on the progress made in achieving the observance of the provisions of the present Covenant falling within the scope of their activities. These reports may include particulars of decisions and recommendations on such implementation adopted by their competent organs.

Article 19

The Economic and Social Council may transmit to the Commission on Human Rights for study and general recommendation or, as appropriate, for information the reports concerning human rights submitted by States in accordance with articles 16 and 17, and those concerning human rights submitted by the specialized agencies in accordance with article 18.

Article 20

The States Parties to the present Covenant and the specialized agencies concerned may submit comments to the Economic and Social Council on any general recommendation under article 19 or reference to such general recommendation in any report of the Commission on Human Rights or any documentation referred to therein.

Article 21

The Economic and Social Council may submit from time to time to the General Assembly reports with recommendations of a general nature and a summary of the information received from the States Parties to the present Covenant and the specialized agencies on the measures taken and the progress made in achieving general observance of the rights recognized in the present Covenant.

Article 22

The Economic and Social Council may bring to the attention of other organs of the United Nations, their subsidiary organs and specialized agencies concerned with furnishing technical assistance any matters arising out of the reports referred to in this part of the present Covenant which may assist such bodies in deciding, each within its field of competence, on the advisability of international measures likely to contribute to the effective progressive implementation of the present Covenant.

Article 23

The States Parties to the present Covenant agree that international action for the achievement of the rights recognized in the present Covenant includes such methods as the conclusion of conventions, the adoption of recommendations, the furnishing of technical assistance and the holding of regional meetings and technical meetings for the purpose of consultation and study organized in conjunction with the Governments concerned.

Article 24

Nothing in the present Covenant shall be interpreted as impairing the provisions of the Charter of the United Nations and of the constitutions of the specialized agencies which define the respective responsibilities of the various organs of the United Nations and of the specialized agencies in regard to the matters dealt with in the present Covenant.

Article 25

Nothing in the present Covenant shall be interpreted as impairing the inherent right of all peoples to enjoy and utilize fully and freely their natural wealth and resources.

Part V

Article 26

1. The present Covenant is open for signature by any State Member of the United Nations or member of any of its specialized agencies, by any State Party to the Statute of the International Court of Justice, and by any other State which has been invited by the General Assembly of the United Nations to become a party to the present Covenant.
2. The present Covenant is subject to ratification. Instruments of ratifi-

cation shall be deposited with the Secretary-General of the United Nations.

3. The present Covenant shall be open to accession by any State referred to in paragraph 1 of this article.

4. Accession shall be effected by the deposit of an instrument of accession with the Secretary-General of the United Nations.

5. The Secretary-General of the United Nations shall inform all States which have signed the present Covenant or acceded to it of the deposit of each instrument of ratification or accession.

Article 27

1. The present Covenant shall enter into force three months after the date of the deposit with the Secretary-General of the United Nations of the thirty-fifth instrument of ratification or instrument of accession.

2. For each State ratifying the present Covenant or acceding to it after the deposit of the thirty-fifth instrument of ratification or instrument of accession, the present Covenant shall enter into force three months after the date of the deposit of its own instrument of ratification or instrument of accession.

Article 28

The provisions of the present Covenant shall extend to all parts of federal States without any limitations or exceptions.

Article 29

1. Any State Party to the present Covenant may propose an amendment and file it with the Secretary-General of the United Nations. The Secretary-General shall thereupon communicate any proposed amendments to the States Parties to the present Covenant with a request that they notify him whether they favour a conference of States Parties for the purpose of considering and voting upon the proposals. In the event that at least one third of the States Parties favours such a conference, the Secretary-General shall convene the conference under the auspices of the United Nations. Any amendment adopted by a majority of the States Parties present and voting at the conference shall be submitted to the General Assembly of the United Nations for approval.

2. Amendments shall come into force when they have been approved by the General Assembly of the United Nations and accepted by a two-thirds majority of the States Parties to the present Covenant in accordance with their respective constitutional processes.

3. When amendments come into force they shall be binding on those States Parties which have accepted them, other States Parties still being

bound by the provisions of the present Covenant and any earlier amendment which they have accepted.

Article 30

Irrespective of the notifications made under article 26, paragraph 5, the Secretary-General of the United Nations shall inform all States referred to in paragraph 1 of the same article of the following particulars:
(a) Signatures, ratifications and accessions under article 26;
(b) The date of the entry into force of the present Covenant under article 27 and the date of the entry into force of any amendments under article 29.

Article 31

1. The present Covenant, of which the Chinese, English, French, Russian and Spanish texts are equally authentic, shall be deposited in the archives of the United Nations.
2. The Secretary-General of the United Nations shall transmit certified copies of the present Covenant to all States referred to in article 26.

3 The International Covenant on Civil and Political Rights

Adopted and opened for signature, ratification and accession by General Assembly Resolution 2200 A (XXI) of 16 December 1966
Entry into Force: 23 March 1976, in Accordance with Article 49

Preamble

The States Parties to the present Covenant,

Considering that, in accordance with the principles proclaimed in the Charter of the United Nations, recognition of the inherent dignity and of the equal and inalienable rights of all members of the human family is the foundation of freedom, justice and peace in the world,

Recognizing that these rights derive from the inherent dignity of the human person,

Recognizing that, in accordance with the Universal Declaration of Human Rights, the ideal of free human beings enjoying civil and political freedom and freedom from fear and want can only be achieved if conditions are created whereby everyone may enjoy his civil and political rights, as well as his economic, social and cultural rights,

Considering the obligation of States under the Charter of the United Nations to promote universal respect for, and observance of, human rights and freedoms,

Realizing that the individual, having duties to other individuals and to the community to which he belongs, is under a responsibility to strive for the promotion and observance of the rights recognized in the present Covenant,

Agree upon the following articles:

Part I

Article 1

1. All peoples have the right of self-determination. By virtue of that right they freely determine their political status and freely pursue their economic, social and cultural development.

2. All peoples may, for their own ends, freely dispose of their natural wealth and resources without prejudice to any obligations arising out of international economic co-operation, based upon the principle of mutual benefit, and international law. In no case may a people be deprived of its own means of subsistence.

3. The States Parties to the present Covenant, including those having responsibility for the administration of Non-Self-Governing and Trust Territories, shall promote the realization of the right of self-determination, and shall respect that right, in conformity with the provisions of the Charter of the United Nations.

Part II

Article 2

1. Each State Party to the present Covenant undertakes to respect and to ensure to all individuals within its territory and subject to its jurisdiction the rights recognized in the present Covenant, without distinction of any kind, such as race, colour, sex, language, religion, political or other opinion, national or social origin, property, birth or other status.

2. Where not already provided for by existing legislative or other measures, each State Party to the present Covenant undertakes to take the necessary steps, in accordance with its constitutional processes and with the provisions of the present Covenant, to adopt such legislative or other measures as may be necessary to give effect to the rights recognized in the present Covenant.

3. Each State Party to the present Covenant undertakes:

(a) To ensure that any person whose rights or freedoms as herein recognized are violated shall have an effective remedy, notwithstanding that the violation has been committed by persons acting in an official capacity;

(b) To ensure that any person claiming such a remedy shall have his right thereto determined by competent judicial, administrative or legislative authorities, or by any other competent authority provided for by the legal

system of the State, and to develop the possibilities of judicial remedy;
(c) To ensure that the competent authorities shall enforce such remedies when granted.

Article 3

The States Parties to the present Covenant undertake to ensure the equal right of men and women to the enjoyment of all civil and political rights set forth in the present Covenant.

Article 4

1. In time of public emergency which threatens the life of the nation and the existence of which is officially proclaimed, the States Parties to the present Covenant may take measures derogating from their obligations under the present Covenant to the extent strictly required by the exigencies of the situation, provided that such measures are not inconsistent with their other obligations under international law and do not involve discrimination solely on the ground of race, colour, sex, language, religion or social origin.
2. No derogation from articles 6, 7, 8 (paragraphs 1 and 2), 11, 15, 16 and 18 may be made under this provision.
3. Any State Party to the present Covenant availing itself of the right of derogation shall immediately inform the other States Parties to the present Covenant, through the intermediary of the Secretary-General of the United Nations, of the provisions from which it has derogated and of the reasons by which it was actuated. A further communication shall be made, through the same intermediary, on the date on which it terminates such derogation.

Article 5

1. Nothing in the present Covenant may be interpreted as implying for any State, group or person any right to engage in any activity or perform any act aimed at the destruction of any of the rights and freedoms recognized herein or at their limitation to a greater extent than is provided for in the present Covenant.
2. There shall be no restriction upon or derogation from any of the fundamental human rights recognized or existing in any State Party to the present Covenant pursuant to law, conventions, regulations or custom on the pretext that the present Covenant does not recognize such rights or that it recognizes them to a lesser extent.

Part III

Article 6

1. Every human being has the inherent right to life. This right shall be protected by law. No one shall be arbitrarily deprived of his life.
2. In countries which have not abolished the death penalty, sentence of death may be imposed only for the most serious crimes in accordance with the law in force at the time of the commission of the crime and not contrary to the provisions of the present Covenant and to the Convention on the Prevention and Punishment of the Crime of Genocide. This penalty can only be carried out pursuant to a final judgement rendered by a competent court.
3. When deprivation of life constitutes the crime of genocide, it is understood that nothing in this article shall authorize any State Party to the present Covenant to derogate in any way from any obligation assumed under the provisions of the Convention on the Prevention and Punishment of the Crime of Genocide.
4. Anyone sentenced to death shall have the right to seek pardon or commutation of the sentence. Amnesty, pardon or commutation of the sentence of death may be granted in all cases.
5. Sentence of death shall not be imposed for crimes committed by persons below eighteen years of age and shall not be carried out on pregnant women.
6. Nothing in this article shall be invoked to delay or to prevent the abolition of capital punishment by any State Party to the present Covenant.

Article 7

No one shall be subjected to torture or to cruel, inhuman or degrading treatment or punishment. In particular, no one shall be subjected without his free consent to medical or scientific experimentation.

Article 8

1. No one shall be held in slavery; slavery and the slave-trade in all their forms shall be prohibited.
2. No one shall be held in servitude.

3(a) No one shall be required to perform forced or compulsory labour;

(b) Paragraph 3 (*a*) shall not be held to preclude, in countries where imprisonment with hard labour may be imposed as a punishment for a crime, the performance of hard labour in pursuance of a sentence to such punishment by a competent court;

(c) For the purpose of this paragraph the term “forced or compulsory labour” shall not include:

(i) Any work or service, not referred to in subparagraph (b), normally required of a person who is under detention in consequence of a lawful order of a court, or of a person during conditional release from such detention;
(ii) Any service of a military character and, in countries where conscientious objection is recognized, any national service required by law of conscientious objectors;
(iii) Any service exacted in cases of emergency or calamity threatening the lifeor well-being of the community;
(iv) Any work or service which forms part of normal civil obligations.

Article 9

1. Everyone has the right to liberty and security of person. No one shall be subjected to arbitrary arrest or detention. No one shall be deprived of his liberty except on such grounds and in accordance with such procedure as are established by law.
2. Anyone who is arrested shall be informed, at the time of arrest, of the reasons for his arrest and shall be promptly informed of any charges against him.
3. Anyone arrested or detained on a criminal charge shall be brought promptly before a judge or other officer authorized by law to exercise judicial power and shall be entitled to trial within a reasonable time or to release. It shall not be the general rule that persons awaiting trial shall be detained in custody, but release may be subject to guarantees to appear for trial, at any other stage of the judicial proceedings, and, should occasion arise, for execution of the judgement.
4. Anyone who is deprived of his liberty by arrest or detention shall be entitled to take proceedings before a court, in order that that court may decide without delay on the lawfulness of his detention and order his release if the detention is not lawful.
5. Anyone who has been the victim of unlawful arrest or detention shall have an enforceable right to compensation.

Article 10

1. All persons deprived of their liberty shall be treated with humanity and with respect for the inherent dignity of the human person.
2(a) Accused persons shall, save in exceptional circumstances, be segregated from convicted persons and shall be subject to separate treatment appropriate to their status as unconvicted persons;
(b) Accused juvenile persons shall be separated from adults and brought as speedily as possible for adjudication.
3. The penitentiary system shall comprise treatment of prisoners the

essential aim of which shall be their reformation and social rehabilitation. Juvenile offenders shall be segregated from adults and be accorded treatment appropriate to their age and legal status.

Article 11

No one shall be imprisoned merely on the ground of inability to fulfil a contractual obligation.

Article 12

1. Everyone lawfully within the territory of a State shall, within that territory, have the right to liberty of movement and freedom to choose his residence.
2. Everyone shall be free to leave any country, including his own.
3. The above-mentioned rights shall not be subject to any restrictions except those which are provided by law, are necessary to protect national security, public order (*ordre public*), public health or morals or the rights and freedoms of others, and are consistent with the other rights recognized in the present Covenant.
4. No one shall be arbitrarily deprived of the right to enter his own country.

Article 13

An alien lawfully in the territory of a State Party to the present Covenant may be expelled therefrom only in pursuance of a decision reached in accordance with law and shall, except where compelling reasons of national security otherwise require, be allowed to submit the reasons against his expulsion and to have his case reviewed by, and be represented for the purpose before, the competent authority or a person or persons especially designated by the competent authority.

Article 14

1. All persons shall be equal before the courts and tribunals. In the determination of any criminal charge against him, or of his rights and obligations in a suit at law, everyone shall be entitled to a fair and public hearing by a competent, independent and impartial tribunal established by law. The press and the public may be excluded from all or part of a trial for reasons of morals, public order (*ordre public*) or national security in a democratic society, or when the interest of the private lives of the parties so requires, or to the extent strictly necessary in the opinion of the court in special circumstances where publicity would prejudice the interests of justice; but any judgement rendered in a criminal case or in a suit at law shall

be made public except where the interest of juvenile persons otherwise requires or the proceedings concern matrimonial disputes or the guardianship of children.

2. Everyone charged with a criminal offence shall have the right to be presumed innocent until proved guilty according to law.

3. In the determination of any criminal charge against him, everyone shall be entitled to the following minimum guarantees, in full equality:

(a) To be informed promptly and in detail in a language which he understands of the nature and cause of the charge against him;

(b) To have adequate time and facilities for the preparation of his defence and to communicate with counsel of his own choosing;

(c) To be tried without undue delay;

(d) To be tried in his presence, and to defend himself in person or through legal assistance of his own choosing; to be informed, if he does not have legal assistance, of this right; and to have legal assistance assigned to him, in any case where the interests of justice so require, and without payment by him in any such case if he does not have sufficient means to pay for it;

(e) To examine, or have examined, the witnesses against him and to obtain the attendance and examination of witnesses on his behalf under the same conditions as witnesses against him;

(f) To have the free assistance of an interpreter if he cannot understand or speak the language used in court;

(g) Not to be compelled to testify against himself or to confess guilt.

4. In the case of juvenile persons, the procedure shall be such as will take account of their age and the desirability of promoting their rehabilitation.

5. Everyone convicted of a crime shall have the right to his conviction and sentence being reviewed by a higher tribunal according to law.

6. When a person has by a final decision been convicted of a criminal offence and when subsequently his conviction has been reversed or he has been pardoned on the ground that a new or newly discovered fact shows conclusively that there has been a miscarriage of justice, the person who has suffered punishment as a result of such conviction shall be compensated according to law, unless it is proved that the non-disclosure of the unknown fact in time is wholly or partly attributable to him.

7. No one shall be liable to be tried or punished again for an offence for which he has already been finally convicted or acquitted in accordance with the law and penal procedure of each country.

Article 15

1. No one shall be held guilty of any criminal offence on account of any act or omission which did not constitute a criminal offence, under national or international law, at the time when it was committed. Nor shall a heavier penalty be imposed than the one that was applicable at the time when the criminal offence was committed. If, subsequent to the commission of the offence, provision is made by law for the imposition of the lighter penalty, the offender shall benefit thereby.

2. Nothing in this article shall prejudice the trial and punishment of any person for any act or omission which, at the time when it was committed, was criminal according to the general principles of law recognized by the community of nations.

Article 16

Everyone shall have the right to recognition everywhere as a person before the law.

Article 17

1. No one shall be subjected to arbitrary or unlawful interference with his privacy, family, home or correspondence, nor to unlawful attacks on his honour and reputation.

2. Everyone has the right to the protection of the law against such interference or attacks.

Article 18

1. Everyone shall have the right to freedom of thought, conscience and religion. This right shall include freedom to have or to adopt a religion or belief of his choice, and freedom, either individually or in community with others and in public or private, to manifest his religion or belief in worship, observance, practice and teaching.

2. No one shall be subject to coercion which would impair his freedom to have or to adopt a religion or belief of his choice.

3. Freedom to manifest one's religion or beliefs may be subject only to such limitations as are prescribed by law and are necessary to protect public safety, order, health, or morals or the fundamental rights and freedoms of others.

4. The States Parties to the present Covenant undertake to have respect for the liberty of parents and, when applicable, legal guardians to ensure the religious and moral education of their children in conformity with their own convictions.

Article 19

1. Everyone shall have the right to hold opinions without interference.

2. Everyone shall have the right to freedom of expression; this right shall include freedom to seek, receive and impart information and ideas of all kinds, regardless of frontiers, either orally, in writing or in print, in the form of art, or through any other media of his choice.

3. The exercise of the rights provided for in paragraph 2 of this article carries with it special duties and responsibilities. It may therefore be subject to certain restrictions, but these shall only be such as are provided by law and are necessary:

(a) For respect of the rights or reputations of others;

(b) For the protection of national security or of public order (*ordre public*), or of public health or morals.

Article 20

1. Any propaganda for war shall be prohibited by law.

2. Any advocacy of national, racial or religious hatred that constitutes incitement to discrimination, hostility or violence shall be prohibited by law.

Article 21

The right of peaceful assembly shall be recognized. No restrictions may be placed on the exercise of this right other than those imposed in conformity with the law and which are necessary in a democratic society in the interests of national security or public safety, public order (*ordre public*), the protection of public health or morals or the protection of the rights and freedoms of others.

Article 22

1. Everyone shall have the right to freedom of association with others, including the right to form and join trade unions for the protection of his interests.

2. No restrictions may be placed on the exercise of this right other than those which are prescribed by law and which are necessary in a democratic society in the interests of national security or public safety, public order (*ordre public*), the protection of public health or morals or the protection of the rights and freedoms of others. This article shall not prevent the imposition of lawful restrictions on members of the armed forces and of the police in their exercise of this right.

3. Nothing in this article shall authorize States Parties to the International Labour Organisation Convention of 1948 concerning Freedom of As-

sociation and Protection of the Right to Organise to take legislative measures which would prejudice, or to apply the law in such a manner as to prejudice, the guarantees provided for in that Convention.

Article 23

1. The family is the natural and fundamental group unit of society and is entitled to protection by society and the State.
2. The right of men and women of marriageable age to marry and to found a family shall be recognized.
3. No marriage shall be entered into without the free and full consent of the intending spouses.
4. States Parties to the present Covenant shall take appropriate steps to ensure equality of rights and responsibilities of spouses as to marriage, during marriage and at its dissolution. In the case of dissolution, provision shall be made for the necessary protection of any children.

Article 24

1. Every child shall have, without any discrimination as to race, colour, sex, language, religion, national or social origin, property or birth, the right to such measures of protection as are required by his status as a minor, on the part of his family, society and the State.
2. Every child shall be registered immediately after birth and shall have a name.
3. Every child has the right to acquire a nationality.

Article 25

Every citizen shall have the right and the opportunity, without any of the distinctions mentioned in article 2 and without unreasonable restrictions:
(a) To take part in the conduct of public affairs, directly or through freely chosen representatives;
(b) To vote and to be elected at genuine periodic elections which shall be by universal and equal suffrage and shall be held by secret ballot, guaranteeing the free expression of the will of the electors;
(c) To have access, on general terms of equality, to public service in his country.

Article 26

All persons are equal before the law and are entitled without any discrimination to the equal protection of the law. In this respect, the law shall prohibit any discrimination and guarantee to all persons equal and effective protection against discrimination on any ground such as race, colour, sex, language, religion, political or other opinion, national or social origin, property, birth or other status.

Article 27

In those States in which ethnic, religious or linguistic minorities exist, persons belonging to such minorities shall not be denied the right, in community with the other members of their group, to enjoy their own culture, to profess and practise their own religion, or to use their own language.

Part IV

Article 28

1. There shall be established a Human Rights Committee (hereafter referred to in the present Covenant as the Committee). It shall consist of eighteen members and shall carry out the functions hereinafter provided.
2. The Committee shall be composed of nationals of the States Parties to the present Covenant who shall be persons of high moral character and recognized competence in the field of human rights, consideration being given to the usefulness of the participation of some persons having legal experience.
3. The members of the Committee shall be elected and shall serve in their personal capacity.

Article 29

1. The members of the Committee shall be elected by secret ballot from a list of persons possessing the qualifications prescribed in article 28 and nominated for the purpose by the States Parties to the present Covenant.
2. Each State Party to the present Covenant may nominate not more than two persons. These persons shall be nationals of the nominating State.
3. A person shall be eligible for renomination.

Article 30

1. The initial election shall be held no later than six months after the date of the entry into force of the present Covenant.
2. At least four months before the date of each election to the Committee, other than an election to fill a vacancy declared in accordance with article 34, the Secretary-General of the United Nations shall address a written invitation to the States Parties to the present Covenant to submit their nominations for membership of the Committee within three months.
3. The Secretary-General of the United Nations shall prepare a list in alphabetical order of all the persons thus nominated, with an indication of the States Parties which have nominated them, and shall submit it to the

States Parties to the present Covenant no later than one month before the date of each election.

4. Elections of the members of the Committee shall be held at a meeting of the States Parties to the present Covenant convened by the Secretary-General of the United Nations at the Headquarters of the United Nations. At that meeting, for which two thirds of the States Parties to the present Covenant shall constitute a quorum, the persons elected to the Committee shall be those nominees who obtain the largest number of votes and an absolute majority of the votes of the representatives of States Parties present and voting.

Article 31

1. The Committee may not include more than one national of the same State.

2. In the election of the Committee, consideration shall be given to equitable geographical distribution of membership and to the representation of the different forms of civilization and of the principal legal systems.

Article 32

1. The members of the Committee shall be elected for a term of four years. They shall be eligible for re-election if renominated. However, the terms of nine of the members elected at the first election shall expire at the end of two years; immediately after the first election, the names of these nine members shall be chosen by lot by the Chairman of the meeting referred to in article 30, paragraph 4.

2. Elections at the expiry of office shall be held in accordance with the preceding articles of this part of the present Covenant.

Article 33

1. If, in the unanimous opinion of the other members, a member of the Committee has ceased to carry out his functions for any cause other than absence of a temporary character, the Chairman of the Committee shall notify the Secretary-General of the United Nations, who shall then declare the seat of that member to be vacant.

2. In the event of the death or the resignation of a member of the Committee, the Chairman shall immediately notify the Secretary-General of the United Nations, who shall declare the seat vacant from the date of death or the date on which the resignation takes effect.

Article 34

1. When a vacancy is declared in accordance with article 33 and if the term of office of the member to be replaced does not expire within six months of the declaration of the vacancy, the Secretary-General of the United Nations shall notify each of the States Parties to the present Covenant, which may within two months submit nominations in accordance with article 29 for the purpose of filling the vacancy.

2. The Secretary-General of the United Nations shall prepare a list in alphabetical order of the persons thus nominated and shall submit it to the States Parties to the present Covenant. The election to fill the vacancy shall then take place in accordance with the relevant provisions of this part of the present Covenant.

3. A member of the Committee elected to fill a vacancy declared in accordance with article 33 shall hold office for the remainder of the term of the member who vacated the seat on the Committee under the provisions of that article.

Article 35

The members of the Committee shall, with the approval of the General Assembly of the United Nations, receive emoluments from United Nations resources on such terms and conditions as the General Assembly may decide, having regard to the importance of the Committee's responsibilities.

Article 36

The Secretary-General of the United Nations shall provide the necessary staff and facilities for the effective performance of the functions of the Committee under the present Covenant.

Article 37

1. The Secretary-General of the United Nations shall convene the initial meeting of the Committee at the Headquarters of the United Nations.

2. After its initial meeting, the Committee shall meet at such times as shall be provided in its rules of procedure.

3. The Committee shall normally meet at the Headquarters of the United Nations or at the United Nations Office at Geneva.

Article 38

Every member of the Committee shall, before taking up his duties, make a solemn declaration in open committee that he will perform his functions impartially and conscientiously.

Article 39

1. The Committee shall elect its officers for a term of two years. They may be re-elected.
2. The Committee shall establish its own rules of procedure, but these rules shall provide, *inter alia,* that:
(a) Twelve members shall constitute a quorum;
(b) Decisions of the Committee shall be made by a majority vote of the members present.

Article 40

1. The States Parties to the present Covenant undertake to submit reports on the measures they have adopted which give effect to the rights recognized herein and on the progress made in the enjoyment of those rights:
(a) Within one year of the entry into force of the present Covenant for the States Parties concerned;
(b) Thereafter whenever the Committee so requests.
2. All reports shall be submitted to the Secretary-General of the United Nations, who shall transmit them to the Committee for consideration. Reports shall indicate the factors and difficulties, if any, affecting the implementation of the present Covenant.
3. The Secretary-General of the United Nations may, after consultation with the Committee, transmit to the specialized agencies concerned copies of such parts of the reports as may fall within their field of competence.
4. The Committee shall study the reports submitted by the States Parties to the present Covenant. It shall transmit its reports, and such general comments as it may consider appropriate, to the States Parties. The Committee may also transmit to the Economic and Social Council these comments along with the copies of the reports it has received from States Parties to the present Covenant.
5. The States Parties to the present Covenant may submit to the Committee observations on any comments that may be made in accordance with paragraph 4 of this article.

Article 41

1. A State Party to the present Covenant may at any time declare under this article that it recognizes the competence of the Committee to receive and consider communications to the effect that a State Party claims that another State Party is not fulfilling its obligations under the present Covenant. Communications under this article may be received and considered only if submitted by a State Party which has made a declaration recogniz-

ing in regard to itself the competence of the Committee. No communication shall be received by the Committee if it concerns a State Party which has not made such a declaration. Communications received under this article shall be dealt with in accordance with the following procedure:

(a) If a State Party to the present Covenant considers that another State Party is not giving effect to the provisions of the present Covenant, it may, by written communication, bring the matter to the attention of that State Party. Within three months after the receipt of the communication the receiving State shall afford the State which sent the communication an explanation, or any other statement in writing clarifying the matter which should include, to the extent possible and pertinent, reference to domestic procedures and remedies taken, pending, or available in the matter;

(b) If the matter is not adjusted to the satisfaction of both States Parties concerned within six months after the receipt by the receiving State of the initial communication, either State shall have the right to refer the matter to the Committee, by notice given to the Committee and to the other State;

(c) The Committee shall deal with a matter referred to it only after it has ascertained that all available domestic remedies have been invoked and exhausted in the matter, in conformity with the generally recognized principles of international law. This shall not be the rule where the application of the remedies is unreasonably prolonged;

(d) The Committee shall hold closed meetings when examining communications under this article;

(e) Subject to the provisions of subparagraph (*c*), the Committee shall make available its good offices to the States Parties concerned with a view to a friendly solution of the matter on the basis of respect for human rights and fundamental freedoms as recognized in the present Covenant;

(f) In any matter referred to it, the Committee may call upon the States Parties concerned, referred to in subparagraph (*b*), to supply any relevant information;

(g) The States Parties concerned, referred to in subparagraph (*b*), shall have the right to be represented when the matter is being considered in the Committee and to make submissions orally and/or in writing;

(h) The Committee shall, within twelve months after the date of receipt ofnotice under subparagraph (*b*), submit a report:

(i) If a solution within the terms of subparagraph (*e*) is reached, the Committee shall confine its report to a brief statement of the facts and of the solution reached;

(ii) If a solution within the terms of subparagraph (*e*) is not reached, the Committee shall confine its report to a brief statement of the facts; the written submissions and record of the oral submissions made by the States

Parties concerned shall be attached to the report. In every matter, the report shall be communicated to the States Parties concerned.

2. The provisions of this article shall come into force when ten States Parties to the present Covenant have made declarations under paragraph 1 of this article. Such declarations shall be deposited by the States Parties with the Secretary-General of the United Nations, who shall transmit copies thereof to the other States Parties. A declaration may be withdrawn at any time by notification to the SecretaryGeneral. Such a withdrawal shall not prejudice the consideration of any matter which is the subject of a communication already transmitted under this article; no further communication by any State Party shall be received after the notification of withdrawal of the declaration has been received by the Secretary-General, unless the State Party concerned has made a new declaration.

Article 42

1(a) If a matter referred to the Committee in accordance with article 41 is not resolved to the satisfaction of the States Parties concerned, the Committee may, with the prior consent of the States Parties concerned, appoint an *ad hoc* Conciliation Commission (hereinafter referred to as the Commission). The good offices of the Commission shall be made available to the States Parties concerned with a view to an amicable solution of the matter on the basis of respect for the present Covenant;

(b) The Commission shall consist of five persons acceptable to the States Parties concerned. If the States Parties concerned fail to reach agreement within three months on all or part of the composition of the Commission, the members of the Commission concerning whom no agreement has been reached shall be elected by secret ballot by a two-thirds majority vote of the Committee from among its members.

2. The members of the Commission shall serve in their personal capacity. They shall not be nationals of the States Parties concerned, or of a State not Party to the present Covenant, or of a State Party which has not made a declaration under article 41.

3. The Commission shall elect its own Chairman and adopt its own rules of procedure.

4. The meetings of the Commission shall normally be held at the Headquarters of the United Nations or at the United Nations Office at Geneva. However, they may be held at such other convenient places as the Commission may determine in consultation with the Secretary-General of the United Nations and the States Parties concerned.

5. The secretariat provided in accordance with article 36 shall also service the commissions appointed under this article.

6. The information received and collated by the Committee shall be made available to the Commission and the Commission may call upon the States Parties concerned to supply any other relevant information.

7. When the Commission has fully considered the matter, but in any event not later than twelve months after having been seized of the matter, it shall submit to the Chairman of the Committee a report for communication to the States Parties concerned:

(a) If the Commission is unable to complete its consideration of the matter within twelve months, it shall confine its report to a brief statement of the status of its consideration of the matter;

(b) If an amicable solution to the matter on tie basis of respect for human rights as recognized in the present Covenant is reached, the Commission shall confine its report to a brief statement of the facts and of the solution reached;

(c) If a solution within the terms of subparagraph (*b*) is not reached, the Commission's report shall embody its findings on all questions of fact relevant to the issues between the States Parties concerned, and its views on the possibilities of an amicable solution of the matter. This report shall also contain the written submissions and a record of the oral submissions made by the States Parties concerned;

(d) If the Commission's report is submitted under subparagraph (*c*), the States Parties concerned shall, within three months of the receipt of the report, notify the Chairman of the Committee whether or not they accept the contents of the report of the Commission.

8. The provisions of this article are without prejudice to the responsibilities of the Committee under article 41.

9. The States Parties concerned shall share equally all the expenses of the members of the Commission in accordance with estimates to be provided by the Secretary-General of the United Nations.

10. The Secretary-General of the United Nations shall be empowered to pay the expenses of the members of the Commission, if necessary, before reimbursement by the States Parties concerned, in accordance with paragraph 9 of this article.

Article 43

The members of the Committee, and of the *ad hoc* conciliation commissions which may be appointed under article 42, shall be entitled to the facilities, privileges and immunities of experts on mission for the United Nations as laid down in the relevant sections of the Convention on the Privileges and Immunities of the United Nations.

Article 44

The provisions for the implementation of the present Covenant shall apply without prejudice to the procedures prescribed in the field of human rights by or under the constituent instruments and the conventions of the United Nations and of the specialized agencies and shall not prevent the States Parties to the present Covenant from having recourse to other procedures for settling a dispute in accordance with general or special international agreements in force between them.

Article 45

The Committee shall submit to the General Assembly of the United Nations, through the Economic and Social Council, an annual report on its activities.

Part V

Article 46

Nothing in the present Covenant shall be interpreted as impairing the provisions of the Charter of the United Nations and of the constitutions of the specialized agencies which define the respective responsibilities of the various organs of the United Nations and of the specialized agencies in regard to the matters dealt with in the present Covenant.

Article 47

Nothing in the present Covenant shall be interpreted as impairing the inherent right of all peoples to enjoy and utilize fully and freely their natural wealth and resources.

Part VI

Article 48

1. The present Covenant is open for signature by any State Member of the United Nations or member of any of its specialized agencies, by any State Party to the Statute of the International Court of Justice, and by any other State which has been invited by the General Assembly of the United Nations to become a Party to the present Covenant.
2. The present Covenant is subject to ratification. Instruments of ratification shall be deposited with the Secretary-General of the United Nations.
3. The present Covenant shall be open to accession by any State referred to in paragraph 1 of this article.
4. Accession shall be effected by the deposit of an instrument of accession with the Secretary-General of the United Nations.
5. The Secretary-General of the United Nations shall inform all States

which have signed this Covenant or acceded to it of the deposit of each instrument of ratification or accession.

Article 49

1. The present Covenant shall enter into force three months after the date of the deposit with the Secretary-General of the United Nations of the thirty-fifth instrument of ratification or instrument of accession.
2. For each State ratifying the present Covenant or acceding to it after the deposit of the thirty-fifth instrument of ratification or instrument of accession, the present Covenant shall enter into force three months after the date of the deposit of its own instrument of ratification or instrument of accession.

Article 50

The provisions of the present Covenant shall extend to all parts of federal States without any limitations or exceptions.

Article 51

1. Any State Party to the present Covenant may propose an amendment and file it with the Secretary-General of the United Nations. The Secretary-General of the United Nations shall thereupon communicate any proposed amendments to the States Parties to the present Covenant with a request that they notify him whether they favour a conference of States Parties for the purpose of considering and voting upon the proposals. In the event that at least one third of the States Parties favours such a conference, the Secretary-General shall convene the conference under the auspices of the United Nations. Any amendment adopted by a majority of the States Parties present and voting at the conference shall be submitted to the General Assembly of the United Nations for approval.
2. Amendments shall come into force when they have been approved by the General Assembly of the United Nations and accepted by a two-thirds majority of the States Parties to the present Covenant in accordance with their respective constitutional processes.
3. When amendments come into force, they shall be binding on those States Parties which have accepted them, other States Parties still being bound by the provisions of the present Covenant and any earlier amendment which they have accepted.

Article 52

1. Irrespective of the notifications made under article 48, paragraph 5, the Secretary-General of the United Nations shall inform all States referred

to in paragraph 1 of the same article of the following particulars:
(a) Signatures, ratifications and accessions under article 48;
(b) The date of the entry into force of the present Covenant under article 49 and the date of the entry into force of any amendments under article 51.

Article 53

1. The present Covenant, of which the Chinese, English, French, Russian and Spanish texts are equally authentic, shall be deposited in the archives of the United Nations.
2. The Secretary-General of the United Nations shall transmit certified copies of the present Covenant to all States referred to in article 48.

4 The Optional Protocol to the International Covenant on Civil and Political Rights

Adopted and Opened for Signature, Ratification and Accession by General Assembly Resolution 2200 A (XXI) of 16 December 1966
Entry into Force: 23 March 1976, in Accordance with Article 9

The States Parties to the present Protocol,

Considering that in order further to achieve the purposes of the International Covenant on Civil and Political Rights (hereinafter referred to as the Covenant) and the implementation of its provisions it would be appropriate to enable the Human Rights Committee set up in part IV of the Covenant (hereinafter referred to as the Committee) to receive and consider, as provided in the present Protocol, communications from individuals claiming to be victims of violations of any of the rights set forth in the Covenant.

Have agreed as follows:

Article 1

A State Party to the Covenant that becomes a Party to the present Protocol recognizes the competence of the Committee to receive and consider communications from individuals subject to its jurisdiction who claim to be victims of a violation by that State Party of any of the rights set forth in the Covenant. No communication shall be received by the Committee if it concerns a State Party to the Covenant which is not a Party to the present Protocol.

Article 2

Subject to the provisions of article 1, individuals who claim that any of their rights enumerated in the Covenant have been violated and who have exhausted all available domestic remedies may submit a written communication to the Committee for consideration.

Article 3

The Committee shall consider inadmissible any communication under the present Protocol which is anonymous, or which it considers to be an abuse of the right of submission of such communications or to be incompatible with the provisions of the Covenant.

Article 4

1. Subject to the provisions of article 3, the Committee shall bring any communications submitted to it under the present Protocol to the attention of the State Party to the present Protocol alleged to be violating any provision of the Covenant.

2. Within six months, the receiving State shall submit to the Committee written explanations or statements clarifying the matter and the remedy, if any, that may have been taken by that State.

Article 5

1. The Committee shall consider communications received under the present Protocol in the light of all written information made available to it by the individual and by the State Party concerned.

2. The Committee shall not consider any communication from an individual unless it has ascertained that:

a. The same matter is not being examined under another procedure of international investigation or settlement;

b. The individual has exhausted all available domestic remedies. This shall not be the rule where the application of the remedies is unreasonably prolonged.

3. The Committee shall hold closed meetings when examining communications under the present Protocol.

4. The Committee shall forward its views to the State Party concerned and to the individual.

Article 6

The Committee shall include in its annual report under article 45 of the Covenant a summary of its activities under the present Protocol.

Article 7

Pending the achievement of the objectives of resolution 1514 (XV) adopted by the General Assembly of the United Nations on 14 December 1960 concerning the Declaration on the Granting of Independence to Colonial Countries and Peoples, the provisions of the present Protocol shall in no way limit the right of petition granted to these peoples by the Charter of the United Nations and other international conventions and instruments under the United Nations and its specialized agencies.

Article 8

1. The present Protocol is open for signature by any State which has signed the Covenant.

2. The present Protocol is subject to ratification by any State which has ratified or acceded to the Covenant. Instruments of ratification shall be deposited with the Secretary-General of the United Nations.

3. The present Protocol shall be open to accession by any State which has ratified or acceded to the Covenant.

4. Accession shall be effected by the deposit of an instrument of accession with the Secretary-General of the United Nations.

5. The Secretary-General of the United Nations shall inform all States which have signed the present Protocol or acceded to it of the deposit of each instrument of ratification or accession.

Article 9

1. Subject to the entry into force of the Covenant, the present Protocol shall enter into force three months after the date of the deposit with the Secretary-General of the United Nations of the tenth instrument of ratification or instrument of accession.

2. For each State ratifying the present Protocol or acceding to it after the deposit of the tenth instrument of ratification or instrument of accession, the present Protocol shall enter into force three months after the date of the deposit of its own instrument of ratification or instrument of accession.

Article 10

The provisions of the present Protocol shall extend to all parts of federal States without any limitations or exceptions.

Article 11

1. Any State Party to the present Protocol may propose an amendment and file it with the Secretary-General of the United Nations. The Secretary-General shall thereupon communicate any proposed amendments to the States Parties to the present Protocol with a request that they notify him whether they favour a conference of States Parties for the purpose of considering and voting upon the proposal. In the event that at least one third of the States Parties favours such a conference, the Secretary-General shall convene the conference under the auspices of the United Nations. Any amendment adopted by a majority of the States Parties present and voting at the conference shall be submitted to the General Assembly of the United Nations for approval.

2. Amendments shall come into force when they have been approved by the General Assembly of the United Nations and accepted by a two-thirds majority of the States Parties to the present Protocol in accordance with their respective constitutional processes.

3. When amendments come into force, they shall be binding on those States Parties which have accepted them, other States Parties still being bound by the provisions of the present Protocol and any earlier amendment which they have accepted.

Article 12

1. Any State Party may denounce the present Protocol at any time by written notification addressed to the Secretary-General of the United Nations. Denunciation shall take effect three months after the date of receipt of the notification by the Secretary-General.

2. Denunciation shall be without prejudice to the continued application of the provisions of the present Protocol to any communication submitted under article 2 before the effective date of denunciation.

Article 13

Irrespective of the notifications made under article 8, paragraph 5, of the present Protocol, the Secretary-General of the United Nations shall inform all States referred to in article 48, paragraph 1, of the Covenant of the following particulars:

(a) Signatures, ratifications and accessions under article 8;

(b) The date of the entry into force of the present Protocol under article 9 and the date of the entry into force of any amendments under article 11;

(c) Denunciations under article 12.

Article 14

1. The present Protocol, of which the Chinese, English, French, Russian and Spanish texts are equally authentic, shall be deposited in the archives of the United Nations.

2. The Secretary-General of the United Nations shall transmit certified copies of the present Protocol to all States referred to in article 48 of the Covenant.

5 The Second Optional Protocol to the International Covenant on Civil and Political Rights, Aiming at the Abolition of the Death Penalty

Adopted and Proclaimed by General Assembly Resolution 44/128 of 15 December 1989

The States Parties to the present Protocol,

Believing that abolition of the death penalty contributes to enhancement of human dignity and progressive development of human rights,

Recalling article 3 of the Universal Declaration of Human Rights, adopted on 10 December 1948, and article 6 of the International Covenant on Civil and Political Rights, adopted on 16 December 1966,

Noting that article 6 of the International Covenant on Civil and Political

Rights refers to abolition of the death penalty in terms that strongly suggest that abolition is desirable,

Convinced that all measures of abolition of the death penalty should be considered as progress in the enjoyment of the right to life,

Desirous to undertake hereby an international commitment to abolish the death penalty,

Have agreed as follows:

Article 1

1. No one within the jurisdiction of a State Party to the present Protocol shall be executed.

2. Each State Party shall take all necessary measures to abolish the death penalty within its jurisdiction.

Article 2

1. No reservation is admissible to the present Protocol, except for a reservation made at the time of ratification or accession that provides for the application of the death penalty in time of war pursuant to a conviction for a most serious crime of a military nature committed during wartime.

2. The State Party making such a reservation shall at the time of ratification or accession communicate to the Secretary-General of the United Nations the relevant provisions of its national legislation applicable during wartime.

3. The State Party having made such a reservation shall notify the SecretaryGeneral of the United Nations of any beginning or ending of a state of war applicable to its territory.

Article 3

The States Parties to the present Protocol shall include in the reports they submit to the Human Rights Committee, in accordance with article 40 of the Covenant, information on the measures that they have adopted to give effect to the present Protocol.

Article 4

With respect to the States Parties to the Covenant that have made a declaration under article 41, the competence of the Human Rights Committee to receive and consider communications when a State Party claims that another State Party is not fulfilling its obligations shall extend to the provisions of the present Protocol, unless the State Party concerned has made a statement to the contrary at the moment of ratification or accession.

Article 5

With respect to the States Parties to the first Optional Protocol to the International Covenant on Civil and Political Rights adopted on 16 December 1966, the competence of the Human Rights Committee to receive and consider communications from individuals subject to its jurisdiction shall extend to the provisions of the present Protocol, unless the State Party concerned has made a statement to the contrary at the moment of ratification or accession.

Article 6

1. The provisions of the present Protocol shall apply as additional provisions to the Covenant.
2. Without prejudice to the possibility of a reservation under article 2 of the present Protocol, the right guaranteed in article 1, paragraph 1, of the present Protocol shall not be subject to any derogation under article 4 of the Covenant.

Article 7

1. The present Protocol is open for signature by any State that has signed the Covenant.
2. The present Protocol is subject to ratification by any State that has ratified the Covenant or acceded to it. Instruments of ratification shall be deposited with the Secretary-General of the United Nations.
3. The present Protocol shall be open to accession by any State that has ratified the Covenant or acceded to it.
4. Accession shall be effected by the deposit of an instrument of accession with the Secretary-General of the United Nations.
5. The Secretary-General of the United Nations shall inform all States that have signed the present Protocol or acceded to it of the deposit of each instrument of ratification or accession.

Article 8

1. The present Protocol shall enter into force three months after the date of the deposit with the Secretary-General of the United Nations of the tenth instrument of ratification or accession.
2. For each State ratifying the present Protocol or acceding to it after the deposit of the tenth instrument of ratification or accession, the present Protocol shall enter into force three months after the date of the deposit of its own instrument of ratification or accession.

Article 9

The provisions of the present Protocol shall extend to all parts of federal States without any limitations or exceptions.

Article 10

The Secretary-General of the United Nations shall inform all States referred to in article 48, paragraph 1, of the Covenant of the following particulars:

a. Reservations, communications and notifications under article 2 of the present Protocol;

b. Statements made under articles 4 or 5 of the present Protocol;

c. Signatures, ratifications and accessions under article 7 of the present Protocol:

d. The date of the entry into force of the present Protocol under article 8 thereof.

Article 11

1. The present Protocol, of which the Arabic, Chinese, English, French, Russian and Spanish texts are equally authentic, shall be deposited in the archives of the United Nations.

2. The Secretary-General of the United Nations shall transmit certified copies of the present Protocol to all States referred to in article 48 of the Covenant.

Appendix 3

International Commission of Jurists: The Tunis Declaration on Reinforcing the Rule of Law and Human Rights 2019[1]

Recalling its Declarations, Resolutions and Conclusions adopted at previous Conferences, including in particular, the Act of Athens on the Rule of Law (1955), the Declaration of Delhi on the Rule of Law in a Free Society (1959), the Law of Lagos (1961), the Resolution of Rio de Janeiro on Executive Action and the Rule of Law (1962), the Declaration of Bangkok (1965), the Declaration of Colombo (1966), the Declaration of Dakar (1967), the Conclusions of Vienna on Human Rights in an Undemocratic World (1977), the Caracas Plan of Action on The Independence of Judges and Lawyers (1989), the Bangalore Declaration concerning Economic, Social and Cultural Rights and the Role of Lawyers (1995), The Cape Town Commitment (1998), the Berlin Declaration on Upholding Human Rights and the Rule of Law in Combating Terrorism (2004), the Geneva Declaration and Plan of Action on Upholding the Rule of Law and the Role of Judges and Lawyers in Times of Crisis (2008), the Declaration on Access to Justice and Right to a Remedy in International Human Rights Systems (2012);

Acknowledging that in 2012 all States recommitted themselves to the Rule of Law at the national and international levels through the unanimous adoption by the UN General Assembly of the Declaration of the High-level Meeting of the General Assembly on the Rule of Law at the National and International Levels;

Concerned however that in recent years there have emerged manifest and widening cracks in the fealty and commitment of States and other powerful actors to the primacy of the Rule of Law and human rights as indispensable to the betterment of the human condition and a dignified life for all people;

Aware that this degradation has been largely driven by a broad questioning of the value of universal human rights, the causes of which are complex, but which has been cynically exploited by authoritarian "populist" leaders and movements and other powerful actors to foment a wider global backlash against the Rule of Law and international human rights law framework;

Insistent that despite these retrograde tendencies, it is critical that the

1 https://www.icj.org/wp-content/uploads/2019/04/Universal-ICJ-The-Tunis-Declaration-Advocacy-2019-ENG.pdf.

Rule of Law and human rights law and standards be developed and harnessed so as to effectively contribute to addressing the great challenges to human life and dignity of our times, including catastrophic climate change and the multifarious and sometimes adverse effects of new digital technologies, especially as applied to communications, artificial intelligence, and surveillance;

The International Commission of Jurists, including its Commissioners, Honorary Members, National Sections and Affiliated Organizations, on the Occasion of its Global Congress held in Tunis on 23–24 March 2019, reaffirms that:

1. The ICJ maintains an unyielding commitment to defend and advance the Rule of Law and the legal protection of civil, cultural, economic, political and social rights, and their protection from attack from any quarter, whether by a State agent, business enterprise, armed group or other organized actor.
2. The Rule of Law, as pronounced in the 1959 Declaration of Delhi, is a dynamic concept for the expansion and fulfilment of which jurists are primarily responsible and which should be employed to safeguard and advance human rights.
3. The Rule of Law is not merely a technical instrument of governance, but is necessarily a normative concept, consisting of principles and correlative standards and subject to progressive development.
4. The Rule of Law is inextricably linked to and interdependent with the protection of human rights, as guaranteed in international law and there can be no full realization of human rights without the operation of the Rule of Law, just as there can be no fully operational Rule of Law that does not accord with international human rights law and standards.
5. The Rule of Law is essential to the proper implementation of other important internationally agreed global priorities, such as environmental protection and sustainable development, which, as the 2030 Agenda for Sustainable Development affirms, must be guided by the purposes and principles of the Charter of the United Nations and grounded in the Universal Declaration of Human Rights and international human rights treaties.
6. Individuals, organizations, public institutions, and business enterprises from all sectors of international and domestic society, public or private, are responsible for and accountable to the Rule of Law.
7. The UN Charter, the Universal Declaration of Human Rights and universal and regional human rights treaties are central pillars of international law and essential for the maintenance of international peace and securi-

ty.

8. All human rights, including civil, cultural, economic, political, and social rights, are universal, indivisible, interdependent, interrelated and must be accorded the same importance and priority.

9. The principles that comprise the Rule of Law include the protection of human rights and, among other elements, the following:

(a) the separation of powers in governance,
(b) law made by democratic institutions applying democratic processes,
(c) the right to participation in decision-making and governance,
(d) the presence of a pluralistic system of political parties and organizations and the holding of periodic free and fair elections based on secret balloting and universal and equal suffrage,
(e) the independence of judges and lawyers, as well as their accountability,
(f) the right to a fair trial by a competent, independent, and impartial tribunal established by law,
(g) the accountability of the military to civilian authorities,
(h) the principle of legality and legal certainty, including that law must be stated with clarity and intelligible to those whom it concerns,
(i) the principle of transparency in governance and the administration of justice,
(j) the functioning of a free, independent, and pluralistic media,
(k) the right to recognition as a person before the law,
(l) the principle of equality, equal protection of the law, and nondiscrimination on the grounds of race, colour, sexual orientation or gender identity, age, gender, religion, language political or other opinion, citizenship, nationality or migration status, national, social or ethnic origin, descent, health status, disability, property, socio-economic status, birth or other status,
(m) the principle of accountability and intolerance of impunity, particularly for serious crimes under international law, and
(n) the right to an effective remedy and reparation for human rights and international humanitarian law violations.

10. The ICJ equally affirms the following as critical to the operation of the Rule of Law and the protection of human rights in a democratic society.

Independence of Judges and Lawyers

11. The independence, impartiality and accountability of the judiciary, as well as the independence of lawyers and prosecutors, are fundamental to the Rule of Law and legal protection of human rights, yet all are fac-

ing heightened challenge from governments and other powerful actors in many countries across all regions of the world.

12. These include laws, policies and practices aimed at: limiting or otherwise undermining the jurisdiction of ordinary courts, including by substituting military or other forms of tribunals that provide deficient independence and fair trial guarantees; undermining the security of tenure of judges; removal or discipline of judges on unjustified grounds or through non-independent or otherwise unfair procedures; directly or indirectly interfering with a judge's decision-making in individual cases, including through legislation imposing mandatory minimum sentences; processes of appointments or promotions of judges that are politicized or otherwise fail to value individual independence; failure of other branches of government to enforce court orders and judgments; depriving judiciaries, legal aid programmes, or prosecution services, of necessary financial and human resources; undermining bar associations or other institutions that protect the independence of the legal profession; unduly interfering with the work of individual independent lawyers, including by sanctioning lawyers for fulfilling their professional duties in cases perceived to be against the government's interests, identifying lawyers with their clients or their clients' causes as a result of discharging their functions, or denying people access to independent lawyers of their choosing; interfering with the independence and objectivity of prosecutors; criticism of the judiciary, legal profession, or prosecution services by members of the executive or legislative branches of government, intended to bring one or more of them into disrepute and thereby undermine public confidence; and otherwise weakening guarantees of judicial independence.

13. Political influence or control of the judiciary, other forms of intimidation or interference by governments or other powerful actors, and the corruption of judges, lawyers or prosecutors, as well as lack of independence of individual judges within a judicial hierarchy, manipulation of assignment of cases, and similar issues of internal independence, have often resulted in the judiciary itself being unable or unwilling to fulfil its role as an independent check on the arbitrary use of power by the executive and legislative branches of government, as an impartial arbiter of disputes between private persons, and as a guarantor of the fair administration of justice and fair trial rights.

14. International and regional organizations, executive (including administrative), legislative, and judicial authorities of every government, and civil society groups, should do everything possible within their respective competencies and capacities to defend and promote the Rule of Law at the international and national levels against the threats identified above.

Such efforts include applying and reinforcing international standards on independence and accountability of judges, lawyers and prosecutors, and human rights in the administration of justice.

15. International legal and other standards for the independence, accountability and appropriate role of judges, lawyers and prosecutors remain at all times vital and their full implementation should be pursued as a matter of urgency, including particularly the right to a fair and public hearing by a competent, independent and impartial tribunal established by law.

16. In every country, provisions of a constitutional nature should provide specific safeguards for judicial independence and accountability and for equal access to independent legal assistance within the framework of an independent legal profession, including enforceable guarantees of free legal aid in accordance with international standards.

17. In addition to elements already recognized in the UN Basic Principles on the Independence of the Judiciary, UN Basic Principles on the Role of Lawyers, and UN Guidelines on the Role of Prosecutors, including the right of judges, lawyers and prosecutors to form professional associations to defend their independence and appropriate roles and to promote the rule of law and legal protection for human rights, effective safeguards can include among other things:

- judicial councils, with at least a majority of their members being judges elected by their peers, and without involvement of the political branches of government, developing and administering fair and transparent grounds and procedures for discipline and removal, or recommendation of removal, of judges and other aspects of the judicial career;
- the adoption and implementation by judiciaries themselves of ethical and professional conduct standards to secure judicial integrity and prevent and respond to judicial corruption and other judicial misconduct including sexual harassment and other forms of discrimination or other judicial involvement in, or inaction in reaction to, violations of human rights.

18. To ensure public confidence and promote human rights values, judiciaries, the legal profession, and prosecution services should reflect the diversity in the societies they serve. All forms of discrimination in the composition of judiciaries, legal profession and prosecution services, as well as in the administration of justice, must be eliminated. In this respect, particular attention is needed to direct or indirect exclusionary discrimination on the basis of such grounds as sex, gender, national or ethnic origin, religion, caste, language, race or sexual orientation, or against persons from

frequently marginalized or disadvantaged groups such as people living in poverty, indigenous peoples, rural populations, refugees and migrants, and persons with disabilities. Continuing legal education for judges, lawyers and prosecutors should be organized by their respective professional associations or similar independent bodies.

19. The ICJ commits to contributing to these objectives by, among other things:

- acting at the national, regional and global levels to support institutional and operational independence of the judiciary, legal profession and prosecution services, and to protect individual judges, lawyers and prosecutors who face attack arising from their work to uphold the Rule of Law or otherwise to protect human rights;
- acting at the national, regional and global levels to promote impartiality of judges and prosecutors and the duty of judges and prosecutors to fulfil their duties in a manner consistent with international law and standards on the Rule of Law and human rights, and to promote appropriate mechanisms to hold judges and prosecutors accountable when they fail to do so;
- challenging, through litigation and other forms of advocacy and legal reform efforts, any legislation, policies or other measures, inconsistent with international standards on the independence or appropriate roles of judges, lawyers or prosecutors; and
- contributing to the work of the United Nations and regional organizations with the aim of developing and strengthening standards relevant to the independence and accountability of judges, lawyers and prosecutors, and their implementation.

Accountability and Access to Justice

20. Accountability and Access to Justice mechanisms organized and pursued in accordance with Rule of Law principles are essential for the protection of human rights. There has been significant progress, in some respects, in ensuring accountability for violations and access to justice to victims in recent times. A series of national mechanisms, and international justice institutions, including those involved in the prosecutions of high-ranking officials, and international institutions such as the International Criminal Court, have been established to advance the fight against impunity and facilitate justice and reparation. Various non-judicial mechanisms have also contributed to accountability and reparation.

21. There is understandable frustration at the pace of progress in fighting impunity around the world. In recent years there have also been increased

attacks on the international accountability and justice framework and institutions, including the International Criminal Court (ICC) and its work. The ICC lacks sufficient political, financial and technical support and cooperation of states, including in executing arrest warrants. Political impasses have made Security Council referrals rare and unlikely. This situation has led to impunity for some of the most serious crimes under international law.

22. Nonetheless, accountability and justice mechanisms and the progress achieved are under persistent attack. During periods of transition, judicial and non-judicial measures can be helpful in revealing the truth, ensuring reparations, facilitating prosecutions and paving the way to institutional reforms, and reconciliation. But in many transitional processes, the Rule of Law is inadequately addressed, perpetuating impunity. Justice and investigative mechanisms face reduced budgets, questions about their efficiency and legitimacy, accusations of bias and threats against judges and court officers and insufficient protections for witnesses. In various countries, accountability and justice components of peace agreements are not implemented or their import limited by legal or judicial decisions that fail to investigate and sanction gross human rights violations and crimes under international law.

23. Access to justice and the right to effective remedies and reparation for human rights violations and abuses are increasingly recognized in principle. Nonetheless, in certain countries accessible, affordable justice is prevented or impeded in practice, as political, financial, procedural and legal barriers persist. The prevalence of corruption in the judiciary undermines access to justice and accountability in many countries.

24. While some national justice systems increasingly use universal and other expansive grounds of jurisdiction to address impunity, and some prosecution services are more willing to investigate and/or prosecute private economic actors' involvement in the commission of crimes abroad, these efforts still remain the exception. The creation of innovative accountability mechanisms such as the International Independent Investigative Mechanisms (IIIMs) is a welcome development.

25. The ICJ reaffirms that it is the obligation of all States to conduct prompt, independent, thorough, transparent and impartial investigations of alleged international human rights and serious international humanitarian law violations, and where appropriate prosecute those responsible in fair trials. Any sentence should be commensurate with the gravity of the offence. Any amnesties or immunities provided which contravene international law and standards should be removed.

26. The duty of States to investigate extends to situations where violations

or abuses have been committed directly or with the participation of business enterprises. In relation to non-State actors, including business actors, States should ensure that they enact legislation holding them accountable for the commission of or participation in violations or abuses, ensuring that their courts are accessible, that trials are fair and that remedy and reparation is effective.

27. All victims of human rights violations have a right to access justice and to an effective remedy and reparations for human rights violations and the State should take prompt action to dismantle barriers with special attention to marginalized and disadvantaged groups. These rights must be able to be exercised at all times, including in times of conflict or transition. States must remove barriers to persons seeking justice against abuses by business enterprises, including through legal and judicial reform. At the international level, this means successful elaboration of legally binding instruments on business and human rights.

28. Respect for Rule of Law principles is essential in the global fight against impunity. This requires that:

- States that have not already done so become party to the Rome Statute of the International Criminal Court (ICC) and accept the Kampala amendment on the crime of aggression – in particular this should be expected of all Members of the Security Council.
- States should effectively cooperate with the ICC, including by executing its arrest warrants and ensuring that it is adequately resourced.
- Members of the United Nations Security Council (UNSC) must apply objective criteria for referring situations to the ICC and refrain from unduly obstructing referrals to the ICC.

29. All States should enable and make the fullest use of the full range of grounds of jurisdiction mandated or permitted under international law, through their national justice systems, including by implementing universal jurisdiction or other expansive forms of jurisdiction to ensure that there is no impunity for crimes under international law. They should allocate adequate resources for administration of justice for such purposes. All States should cooperate with other States and international organizations in the investigation and prosecution of crimes under international law in fair trials and enforcement of sentences, including by facilitating mutual legal assistance and extradition in line with international human rights law and standards.

30. The ICJ will continue to support and advocate for:

- Effective accountability and justice institutions, including the ICC, at the global, regional and national levels and collaboration with others in the same effort;

- Protection of national law enforcement and prosecution authorities against interference and their empowerment to enforce international criminal law obligations;
- Effective implementation of decisions of national, regional, and global judicial bodies;
- The establishment of effective regional mechanisms, where they do not exist, and the strengthening and protection of existing mechanisms; and
- The creation of additional mechanisms, for which there is a pressing need, including a world human rights court, to provide access to justice for human rights violations at the universal level and an effective treaty on business and human rights. Other needed mechanisms include an international permanent standing Independent Investigative Mechanism, or at least ad hoc mechanisms where needed to gather and preserve evidence of crimes under international law, particularly in respect of situations where there are not yet international or domestic judicial mechanisms able or willing to administer justice.

Security and the Rule of Law

31. Fifteen years after the ICJ issued its Berlin Declaration the world faces heightened and new challenges to the Rule of Law and human rights because of States' responses to terrorism and other security challenges. Well-established and cherished legal principles continue to be called into question in all regions of the world. Resort to ill-conceived responses to terrorism and to new security threats continues, undermining the Rule of Law and human rights protections, without compelling scientific evidence that those responses actually work.

32. States continue to shift from criminal law based responses to administrative means to address real and purported security challenges, with far reaching consequences but less human rights protection. Recourse to states of exception has severely diminished or deprived persons of their rights protection under the Rule of Law. So-called exceptional measures – such as the use of indefinite detention and internment without charge or trial, special courts, and extended jurisdiction of military tribunals – have often been announced as temporary but have become permanent in law or in practice. At times, some States have resorted to extrajudicial executions, including by targeted killings, under the pretence of countering terrorism.

33. Governments adopting xenophobic, authoritarian or extreme nationalistic policies have expanded resort to these forms of exception in order to suppress human rights defenders and other civil society, political oppo-

sition, migrants, refugees, stateless persons, minorities or other persons exercising their human rights and fundamental freedoms. Those persons who are marginalized are arbitrarily targeted by authorities and the media and designated as 'security threats'.

34. Recourse to overly broad notions of 'violent extremism', terrorism, sedition, rebellion and 'hate speech', and to vaguely defined preparatory or ancillary offences far removed from any violent act of terrorism, erode the principle of legality and in some cases effectively criminalize the exercise of freedoms of expression, assembly, association and political participation.

35. Rapid technological advancements, including the use of "big data", have given States greater capacity to conduct invasive, targeted and wide-scale surveillance. This has far-reaching impacts on almost all human rights offline and online, particularly the right to privacy, including through pervasive powers to regulate online content and prosecute a range of expression. The push by States for supremacy of security over other interests includes pressure on private service providers to take steps that unnecessarily or disproportionately interfere with human rights.

36. The ICJ condemns terrorism and affirms that all States have an obligation to take effective measures against terrorism, including for the purposes of protecting human rights. No grievances can justify terrorist acts or inflicting terror on the population. Those individuals and groups that commit terrorist acts, crimes under international law and gross human rights abuses must be held accountable.

37. The ICJ reaffirms the centrality of the Rule of Law and human rights in upholding the right to security of all people. Security and human rights are not conflicting objectives but are complementary and mutually reinforcing. In contrast, violations of the Rule of Law and of human rights are conducive to the spread of terrorism or other crimes.

38. The ICJ reaffirms that any resort to the use of force by a State outside its borders in the territory of another State must be undertaken in conformity with its obligations under the UN Charter.

39. The ICJ commits to continue to promote the centrality of the ordinary criminal justice system and of an independent and impartial judiciary in countering security threats. It will act to ensure that the basic principles of legality, necessity and proportionality are fully respected.

40. The ICJ will oppose *de jure or de facto* states of exception without legal mechanisms in place to ensure their temporary, necessary, proportionate and non-discriminatory nature, in line with the standards enshrined in the derogation clauses of international human rights treaties.

41. The ICJ will oppose the use of security and counter-terrorism laws

and practices to suppress human rights defenders, civil society, political opposition, marginalized or disadvantaged groups within their societies, or other persons expressing dissent.

42. The ICJ will work to ensure that the rights of people offline be protected also online, including through a strong international legal framework of responsibility for human rights violations and abuses in the cyber-sphere.

43. The ICJ will continue to call on States, international organizations, businesses and other private entities to align their security strategies and regulatory frameworks with the Rule of Law and international law. Similarly, the ICJ will urge that judges, prosecutors, lawyers and all justice sector actors worldwide, including in their work related to global security, meet their responsibilities as defenders of the Rule of Law and of internationally protected human rights.

Equality and Non-Discrimination

44. Worldwide, increasing attacks on the rule of law have intensified longstanding inequalities and compounded intersecting forms of discrimination against women and girls and persons from marginalized groups. This has limited their enjoyment of human rights and their effective access to justice. States and non-State actors driven by extreme religious, nationalistic, authoritarian or xenophobic ideologies have directed hostile rhetoric at already disadvantaged groups within their societies, fomenting division, stigma, discrimination and even violence. In many countries, culture, tradition, or religion are being used to justify laws, policies and practices that discriminate against women and girls, migrants, refugees, ethnic, religious, sexual or gender minorities, and others based on their status.

45. This occurs at a time when growing economic inequality, accelerating climate change, conflict and large-scale displacement of people, pose grave risks to the protection of human rights. These risks are compounded by the barriers people living in poverty face in accessing justice, such as lack of access to information about their rights, including through digital technology, and the resulting inability to access the remedies they need. Among those living in poverty, it is women, children, older persons, persons with disabilities, migrants, refugees, indigenous people, racial, ethnic, religious groups, sexual or gender minorities, or those stigmatized on grounds of caste, language, or health status, who are likely to be most impeded in accessing justice. National constitutions, laws and jurisprudence, as well as allocation of public resources, are often inadequate to ensure that the justice system is accessible and effective in protecting human rights.

46. The ICJ recognizes the persistent, deep entrenchment of patriarchal culture that perpetuates gender stereotypes in many national and international institutions, including those of the legal profession and the judiciary. Such stereotypes restrict women and girls' enjoyment of their human rights and equal access to justice, including for crimes of sexual and gender-based violence. Sexual harassment, violence, bullying and discrimination against women in the workplace, both nationally and internationally, including in the legal profession and the judiciary, have not been sufficiently addressed. Too often, laws that aim to protect women's rights do not comply with international law and standards, or their implementation is poor or non-existent or insufficiently resourced.
47. In many countries, increasing resort to the criminal law has a discriminatory impact. Laws criminally sanctioning consensual, non-exploitative sexual conduct, sexual and reproductive healthcare services including abortion, personal drug use and HIV, have a detrimental impact on health, equality and human rights, particularly for women, girls and sexual and gender minorities. Criminalization of freedom of expression contrary to international human rights law, including through "blasphemy" laws, violates, in particular, the rights of those belonging to minority religions or beliefs as well as non-believers.
48. In accordance with the principles of the universality of human rights, and of non-discrimination, equality and equal protection, under international law, people are entitled to respect, protection and fulfilment of their human rights, irrespective of race, colour, sexual orientation or gender identity, age, gender, religion, language, political or other opinion, citizenship, nationality or migration status, national, social or ethnic origin, descent, health status, disability, property, socio-economic status, birth or other status. Multi-level, intersecting and compounding forms of discrimination exacerbate and influence the nature of disadvantage, particularly for those living in poverty.
49. International law requires States to implement measures to ensure accessibility, affordability and fairness of justice systems to all. In this regard, the ICJ affirms its commitment:

- Not to discriminate on any grounds in its activities and policies; to value the contributions of all those facing discrimination, and to ensure their meaningful participation;
- To advance realization of the human rights of the most marginalized and excluded, through implementation of international human rights law in national law and practice, including by capacity building for judges, lawyers, and civil society, and dissemination and promotion

of information on international human rights law, aiming to leave no one behind;

- To advocate for justice systems to provide equal access to justice, effective remedies and redress for all without discrimination; to ensure that particular measures are put in place enabling access to justice for women, children, people living in poverty and other marginalized individuals or groups;
- To work to eliminate gender-based discrimination, in particular genderbased violence, gender stereotypes and bias, and sexual harassment including within and by the judiciary and the legal profession;
- To work for the repeal of laws that have a discriminatory impact, in particular laws that criminalize consensual, non-exploitative sexual conduct; sexual and reproductive healthcare, including abortion; personal drug use or possession; HIV non-disclosure, exposure or transmission; or freedom of expression concerning religion or belief.

50. The ICJ urges judges and lawyers worldwide to meet their responsibilities to uphold the universal and equal protection of human rights for all, in particular those subject to discrimination in national laws, policies or practices; to work to ensure the full implementation in national legal systems of the rights of those groups threatened by discriminatory laws or policies; and to work to end entrenched discrimination and discriminatory stereotypes and bias.

Civil Society Space and Fundamental Freedoms

51. In recent years, there has emerged a trend towards closing civil society space, raising profound concerns for the preservation of the Rule of Law, and the protection of an international legal order. In some countries, including those perceived or self-identified as democratic, this degradation has been achieved through increased regulation and surveillance, prosecution, violence, threats or intimidation. The rise of extreme forms of nationalism and authoritarian populism has contributed to widespread censorship, misinformation and an impoverished public discourse on human rights.

52. The protection of the human rights to freedoms of expression, association and assembly has also been sharply eroded. Governments have framed civil society as agents of unfriendly governments or as "enemies of the people". Persecution of human rights defenders, political opponents, journalists and prodemocracy activists has also increased – including extrajudicial killings, enforced disappearances, arbitrary arrest and detention, torture and ill-treatment, and failure to protect from attacks and intimidation by non-State actors.

53. Governments have become adept at abusing legal frameworks and invoking distorted notions of the Rule of Law as cover for repressive and regressive policies. Legal threats and harassment have included restrictive NGO laws, or the enforcement of existing law in a biased or politically motivated manner. Laws in diverse areas such as cyber crimes, taxes, money-laundering, and defamation are now as likely to be used to restrict civil society action as laws on national security, counter-terrorism and states of emergency. There is also an increase in unwarranted regulation or outright criminalization of expression online.
54. Governments, particularly their security sectors, have sought to undermine the independence of judiciaries and prosecutors, as well as national human rights institutions and ombudspersons' offices, to gain cover for the consolidation of political power. In various instances, prosecutors and judges have abdicated their professional responsibilities and are used as a tool to persecute human rights defenders, political opponents, and journalists. Civil society efforts to seek effective remedies from international mechanisms have faced obstacles.
55. Elections, and sound legal frameworks governing the democratic process are necessary for the functioning of the Rule of Law and observance of human rights obligations – but they are not sufficient. Political and civic participation are essential for the strengthening of the Rule of Law, which cannot be left to political parties and government representatives alone. This engagement is a key component to the right to political participation protected under international human rights law and standards. Civic engagement is a pre-requisite for the effective reform of Rule of Law institutions. Civil society's independent monitoring role is essential to all aspects of democratic governance.
56. States have obligations to respect, protect and fulfil the rights to all fundamental freedoms, including freedom of expression and opinion, freedom of assembly, freedom of association and the right to political participation. States have particular responsibilities in protecting and facilitating the work of human rights defenders and to provide the necessary conditions for civil society and individuals to freely participate in matters of public interest.
57. Heightened attention must be given to the development of legal frameworks governing new technologies, particularly information technology and social media, to ensure that they incorporate human rights and Rule of Law principles. Political and social discourse increasingly takes place online, and it is imperative that existing legal frameworks are updated, and new ones developed that respect human rights.
58. The ICJ commits itself to addressing obstacles to the implementation

of international law and standards affecting civil society and the protection of human rights and fundamental freedoms.

59. The ICJ will promote standards and models for transparency and effective participation by civil society and individuals at the national and international levels, including in relation to processes for selection and monitoring of judges and other justice actors in line with the principle of the independence of the judiciary; as well as in relation to national human rights institutions and other institutions that promote and protect human rights; and in the design and implementation of human rights compliant public policies.

60. The ICJ will take a broad approach to addressing human rights and fundamental freedoms and civic space, with the aim of integrating legal and other approaches. Empowering lawyers and civil society and human rights defenders must be augmented by engagement with political actors including parliamentarians, not only for purposes of legal reform, but also when enforcement of judicial decisions become problematic, or where judiciaries cannot protect human rights and fundamental freedoms.

Further Reading

Gudmundur Alfredsson and Asbjörn Eide (Eds.), *The Universal Declaration of Human Rights*. The Hague, Kluwer Law International, 1999.

S. J. Anaya, *International Human Rights and Indigenous Peoples*. New York, Aspen, 2009.

J. Becker, *Campaigning for Justice: Human Rights Advocacy in Practice*. Stanford, Stanford University Press, 2013.

S.R.S. Bedi, *The Development of Human Rights Law by the Judges of the International Court of Justice*. Oxford, Hart Publishing, 2007.

Grainne de Burca, *Reframing Human Rights in a Turbulent Era*. Oxford, Oxford University Press, 2021.

T. Buergenthal, "The Normative and Institutional Evolution of International Human Rights", 19 *Human Rights Quarterly* (1997), pp.703–723.

C.P. Cohen, *Jurisprudence of the Committee on the Rights of the Child*. 4 Vols. New York, Transnational Publishers, 2003.

Andrew Clapham, *Human Rights. A Very Short Introduction*. Oxford, Oxford University Press, 2007. Second Edition, 2015.

Andrew Clapham, *The 1949 Geneva Conventions. A Commentary*. Oxford, Oxford University Press, 2015.

A. Conte and R. Burchill, *Defining Civil and Political Rights. The Jurisprudence of the United Nations Human Rights Committee*. Second Edition. Ashgate, 2009.

P. van Dijk, F. van Hoof, A. van Rijn, and L. Zwaak, (Eds.), *Theory and Practice of the European Convention on Human Rights*. Fourth Edition. Antwerp/Oxford, Intersentia, 2006.

G. Dutere, *Key Case Law Extracts: European Court of Human Rights*. Strasbourg, Council of Europe Publishing, 2003.

M. Evans and R. Murray (Eds.), *The African Charter on Human and Peoples' Rights: The System in Practice 1986–2006*. Cambridge, Cambridge University Press, 2008.

H. Fernandez-Ledesma, *The Inter-American System for the Protection of Human Rights*. San José, Costa Rica, Inter-American Institute of Human Rights, 2007.

C. Flinterman, E.V.O. Dankwa, and M. Hamalengwa, *The International Law of Human Rights in Africa: Basic Documents*. The Hague, Kluwer Law International, 1988.

Mary Ann Glendon, *A World Made New. Eleanor Roosevelt and the Universal Declaration of Human Rights*. Random House, 2001.

Yash Ghai and Jill Cottrell (Eds.) *The Role of Judges in Implementing Economic, Social and Cultural Rights*. London, Interights, 2004.

Yash Ghai and Jill Cottrell, *The Millennium Declaration, Rights and Constitutions*. Oxford India, 2011.

D. Gomien, D. Harris, L. Zwaak, *Law and Practice of the European Convention on Human Rights and the European Social Charter*. Strasbourg, Council of Europe Publishing, 1998.

Louis Henkin (Ed.) *The International Bill of Rights*. New York, Columbia University Press, 1981.

Louis Henkin, *The Age of Rights*, New York, Columbia University Press, 1990.

J. Humphrey, *Human Rights. A Great Adventure*. New York, Transnational Publishers, 1984.

International Commission of Jurists, *International Principles on the Independence and Accountability of Judges, Lawyers and Prosecutors. A Practitioners' Guide*. (2004).

N. Jayawickrama, *The Judicial Application of Human Rights Law. National, Regional and International Jurisprudence*. Cambridge, Cambridge University Press, 2002.

E. Klein (Ed.) *The Monitoring System of Human Rights Treaty Obligations*. Berlin, Berlin Verlag, 1998.

Paul Gordon Lauren, *The Evolution of International Human Rights. Visions Seen*. Second Edition. Philadelphia, University of Pennsylvania Press, 2003.

Theodor Meron, *Human Rights and Humanitarian Norms as Customary Law*. Oxford, Clarendon Press, 1989.

Theodor Meron, *Human Rights Law-Making in the United Nations: A Critique of Instruments and Process*. Oxford, Oxford University Press, 1986.

Theodor Meron, *Human Rights in International Law. Legal and Policy Issues* Oxford, Oxford University Press, 1986.

Ginevra Le Moli, *Human Dignity in International Law*. Cambridge, Cambridge University Press, 2021.

Habib C. Malik (Ed.) *The Challenge of Human Rights. Charles Malik and the Universal Declaration*. Beirut, Charles Malik Foundation, 2000.

Frederic Megret and Philip Alston (Eds.), *The United Nations and Human Rights. A Critical Appraisal*. Oxford, Oxford University Press, 2020.

J. Th. Möller and A. de Zayas, *United Nations Human Rights Committee Case Law 1977–2008*. Kehl, N.P. Engel Publisher, 2009

Johannes Morsink, *The Universal Declaration of Human Rights. A Drafting History*. Philadelphia, University of Pennsylvania Press, 1999.

M. Nowak and E. McArthur, *The United Nations Convention Against Torture*. Oxford, Oxford University Press, 2008.

M. O'Flaherty, *Human Rights and the UN: Practice Before the Treaty Bodies*. Second Edition. The Hague, Kluwer Law International, 2002.

T.S. Orlin, A. Rosas, and M. Scheinin, *The Jurisprudence of Human Rights Law. A Comparative Interprettive Approach.* Institute for Human Rights, Abo Akademi University, Turku/Abo, 2000.

J.M. Pasqualucci, *The Practice and Procedure of the Inter-American Court of Human Rights,* Second Edition. Cambridge, Cambridge University Press, 2012.

Pathfinders, *Justice for All. The Task Force on Justice. Final Report.* www.justice.sdg16.plus

Bertrand G. Ramcharan, Theodoor C. Van Boven, Abdul Koroma and Ines French (Eds.), *The Universality of Human Rights. A Handbook.* Leiden, Brill/Nijhoff, 2023.

Bernadette Rainey, Pamela McCormick, and Claire Ovey, *Jacobs, White, and Ovey: The European Convention on Human Rights.* Oxford, Oxford University Press, 2020.

Egon Schwelb, *Crimes Against Humanity.* Oxford, Oxford University Press, 1946.

Bruno Simma, "The International Court of Justice", in Frederic Megret and Philip Alston (Eds.), *The United Nations and Human Rights. A Critical Appraisal.* Oxford, Oxford University Press, 2020, Chapter 4, pp. 151–180.

L. Swepston, Supervision of ILO Standards, 13 *International Journal of Comparative Labour Law,* 1997, pp. 327–344.

Paul M. Taylor, *A Commentary on the International Covenant on Civil and Political Rights.* Cambridge, Cambridge University Press, 2020.

Jay Winter and Antoine Prost, *René Cassin and Human Rights: From the Great War to the Universal Declaration.* Cambridge, Cambridge University Press, 2013.

Index

www.ingramcontent.com/pod-product-compliance
Lightning Source LLC
Chambersburg PA
CBHW041645260925
33220CB00009B/75
9789083407548